Dearest Hannah,

Love to.

deep appreciation
for your feedback
& support.

Love

Cheryl

In 2009, during my last year of seminary at Boston University School of Theology, I started this book. My dream was to combine my theological training and vast experience as a diversity consultant to provide a resource for leaders, especially faith leaders, to facilitate dialogues among people of different races about racism, to enable us, together, to overcome racism. Returning to the book many times, but never finishing it, I was certain the moment for the book's usefulness had passed. Then 2020 hit with the sin-demic of COVID19, obvious evidence of systemic racism, the public murder of George Floyd by law enforcement officers, an economic earthquake with after-shocks still to be realized, and the sharp divide of people communicating in echo chambers. The persistent nudge to build a case for transformative dialogue as a tool to eliminate systemic racism was impossible to ignore.

"God, most high, of great compassion, long suffering and mercy, in whom there is life, and wisdom and love, you are good to all and compassionate over all you have made. Amen."
-W.E.B. Du Bois[i]

Table of Contents

INTRODUCTION

On the morning of October 23, 2013, the church sexton called me at home. The conversation went like this:

Sexton: "Hello, ah, Pastor Cheryl, good morning; good morning. Well, uhhmmm– have you seen it? I mean has anyone called you? I just got to the church and..."

Me: "Hi Dick, how are you? What is it? I haven't seen anything."

Sexton: "Well, oh, I don't know. It's.... well ... someone spray-painted the dumpster that's in the church parking lot. Uhmmm... I just happened to stop by the church and I saw it. I don't know how to say this, but it has a message on it. I've already called the company to have it taken away."

Me: "Wait, Dick, please tell me what is the message? It's okay to read it to me. What was written on the dumpster?"

Sexton: "Well, I hate to say it."

Me: "It's ok- just tell me what it says."

Sexton: "Someone wrote- 'I hate Nigs...' They didn't finish that last word because the writing is so big. I feel terrible. I've called the dumpster company to have it removed. This is just terrible."

Me: "Oh, my! Yes, it is terrible. Thank you for telling me. I know it wasn't easy to make this call and I appreciate you doing so. But, please, don't have it removed. I'm coming to the church now to see it for myself."

I arrived at the church and saw:

It's one thing to hear about it and quite another to have your eyes and soul assaulted by the words. There, in plain sight, a declaration of hatred and bigotry. I would be disingenous if I didn't say I felt hurt, shocked, dehumanized. After calling the police, I made two phone calls to trusted friends who are also clergy. On the heels of those supportive conversations and prayers, I knew this was an opportunity to take what was meant for evil and use it for good. Since the author chose to place his (we later learned it was a local resident) sentiments on the trash dumpster, which is where those sentiments and beliefs belong, I decided to have a "Dump" Prayer Vigil.

We appealed to the love within each of us, and invited the community to join in praying in solidarity against racism. In just four days, the church and I planned the "Dump" Prayer vigil. and received an outpouring of attendees on October 27th. The response from local clergy, community leaders, residents and colleagues in the American Baptist denomination was immediate.

Our plan for the vigil was to open with a general prayer, followed by attendees' own declaration of biases that needed to be thrown into the dump. Understanding that bias is universal

2

and racism persists, attendees would be encouraged to confront an "ism" by writing it on a sticky note; "isms" such as sexism, racism, ableism, heterosexism, ethnocentrism, etc. After that we would leave the sanctuary and go to the dumpster in the parking lot to place the "isms" over the spray-painted message. All of the trash, including the dumpster would subsequently be taken away to the landfill.

That was the plan, spiritual, symbolic and done in solidarity. But it didn't happen that way. The day before the "Dump" Prayer Vigil, the dumpster was removed. On Sunday, instead of the defaced dumpster, a shiny, unmarked new one was in its place. Despite numerous conversations with involved parties to leave the dumpster in place until Monday, someone had it removed. We never learned who authorized the removal.

Nonetheless, the vigil illustrated community solidarity at the standing-room-only "dump" prayer vigil. Attendees affirmed all humans are created equal, loved by God and are to dwell in unity. Moreover, the incident galvanized the church. It expedited the developing relationship between pastor and congregation. "This is our pastor," church members universally expressed. For nearly a decade, First Baptist Church in Attleboro (FBCA), whose demographics matched that of the city, (92% White; 6% Latinx; 2% Black) and I, their first Black, female, settled pastor partnered in ministry. We shone a beaming light on how to listen, learn and love one another.

Upon my retirement in 2020, in place of a physical gathering due to COVID19 distancing guidelines, the congregation created a video montage of messages from church members, family and friends. From the members, the combined tri-fold message was: they grew spiritually, deepened their biblical knowledge and expanded their understanding of diversity. Given the ministry God has called me to, I was and am overjoyed to receive affirmation of God's Calling on my life.

3

It takes emotional courage to confront the ugliness and violence of racism. We have to face it to fix it. As James Baldwin reminds us, "not everything that is faced can be changed, but nothing can be changed until it is faced."

Overall, the incident reinforced the need for dialogues among the church and wider community. It started a conversation within the church that expanded into the community and gained strength in 2020, after the murder of George Floyd.

In addition to serving at FBCA, I also served as covenant pastor at two Massachusetts congregations: West Acton Baptist Church and First Baptist Church of Sharon. All of the congregations are predominately White and they taught me how essential it is for pastors and leaders in general, to allow love to fuel the courage of their convictions and not shrink in the face of resistance. Preaching about racial injustice is downright scary when congregants hear it as an indictment against them. Engaging in small group dialogues challenges all to be courageous, vulnerable and transparent.

In this age when facts are often in dispute, compulsion, force, or argument will not win the day. Relationship, connection, and shared values are the tools of change. No matter how ingrained, or embedded racial injustice is, we don't have to accept things as they are. We have the power to invest ourselves in making the change the world needs.

In this book, you will find a combination of stories, theories and some workbook materials. May these begin to deepen understanding of how to engage in transformative dialogue. May these help us listen and learn our way to the beloved community.

Objectives of this Book

Talk ain't cheap. It's creative. If you don't believe it, just read Genesis 1: ",,, and God said..." From the word spoken, creation was formed. Good conversation for me is formative action. As we listen, truly listen to one another, and open ourselves to consider long-held beliefs that may not be completely true, the seed of change and possibilities for transformation is nurtured.

No. Conversation isn't a passive workaround to avoid change. It is the impetus for change. Dialogue is the one unique quality human beings have above any of God's creations. We are capable of reasoning together with one another. Yes. Conversation can be used to filibuster, delay action, yet when conversation is combined with a desire to understand, a willingness to see through the eyes of another, and a commitment to dialogue, then transformed thinking can emerge.

Transformative dialogue for me is a tool toward building a beloved community. The power of dialogue lies in deep listening and a desire to understand before seeking to be understood. To know what we hear is distinctly different from hearing what we know. To know what we hear requires listening to others. To hear what we know requires nothing of us. In order to listen deeply, participants must suspend individual certainty, question assumptions and view different as different and not deficient. Doing so can result in shared meaning and even a transformed way of thinking.

The beloved community contains no others, simply all of us, living with and among one another. Our ability to listen, consider and respond has the vast potential to close the racial divide between people and foster the beloved community.

This book focuses explicitly but not exclusively, on the relationship between two indigenous cultures of the USA: Black and White people. Quoting Emerson, "White U.S. culture is no more American than Black U.S. culture. Both have been present since the nation's founding."[ii] Baked into the ideological cake of our society is the perspective that Black persons are things to be used, inferior beings, and not full persons. Persistently palpable anti-Black sentiment is one of the reasons White persons are dismayed when confronted with disparate and abusive treatment of Black persons. Like fish swimming in the water, they no longer see the violent assaults of Black and Brown bodies. When all eyes were transfixed on the murder of George Floyd in May 2020 by a law enforcement officer, White persons couldn't avoid seeing, and when they did, "I am shocked!" was a common refrain. Black persons were not shocked. Sad, devastated, angry, but not shocked, because this was more of the same. The fact that White persons, in large numbers, saw the horror as unusual says everything about how Black persons' experiences do not register as meaningful.

Our task as caring persons is to help us see one another as persons. Dialogue is a primary way to accomplish that task. In dialogue each voice is respected and given space for full expression. Dialogue is not debate, rather a reflective learning process designed to examine ideas– and not to coerce – a point of view. Dialogue invites transformation but does not force it. When you consider that racist policies are rooted in racist ideas, exploring and assessing the ideas can be the guide path to belovedness.

However, this book is not exclusively about Black and White populations. As you will see, all Black, Indigenous, People of Color (BIPOC) experience a stance of otherness. Together, BIPOC and White persons are linked in a web of shared humanity that cries out for a bigger "We." A "We" that is acknowledged, respected and embraced. The "We" that God created to love, help and benefit one another.

My vision is that through dialogue, people will join together like some of the best matchups in sports to defeat systemic racial injustice.

Basketball players Larry Bird and Magic Johnson hated each other and now enjoy a legendary friendship. Other basketball legends, Shaquille and Kobe found that team was much more effective than "me". Rivalries between these masterful athletes made them better, stronger and more effective. Continuing to hold animus is nearly impossible when you're in the same game, learning from one another and admiring each other's accomplishments. These rivals becoming friends is no mystery, like them, we too are on the same playing field in life.

This book is meant to be lived; to open into the experience of a whole life in community through the effective, structured tool of dialogue. Leaders, both in the faith community and in society at large, who seek to help communities capitalize on the benefits of their neighbors to eliminate systemic racial oppression – what I call "eracism" – are invited to read this book.

Transformative dialogue facilitates a shared mutual understanding, as participants listen to and learn from each other, rather than debate and argue fixed positions. Transformative dialogue has the potential to re-balance power so that it is shared equitably. We are in this society together and together we must navigate a way to live that celebrates humanity. In dialogue we avoid aggressively defending our position in the attempt to persuade others. Rather, we let our inquiry of others (asking open-ended questions) emerge from a deep place of wonderment within us.

The four objectives I will address include: 1) To unblind eyes that no longer see; 2) to debunk the pervasive myth that we cannot eracism in our lifetimes; 3) to inspire those who deny racism exists to search their hearts; 4) both to learn to love one another and to love learning about one another so that all can benefit equitably in the beloved community. I will elaborate.

1. *To unblind eyes that no longer see.* Just as fish don't see the water in which they are swimming, we don't see systems of racial injustice in our operating norms, practices, policies, because it is a natural part of our existence. For example, when a higher number of Black and Brown students are not reading at grade level, we overlook the operating norm that emphasizes only one right way to teach. Rather, we tacitly blame the children by indicating they have an achievement gap. In reality, it is a cultural instruction gap. With a little awareness, we can increase our sight, notice the ways in which systemic racism lives and moves with and among us, and seek alternatives to eracism.

2. *To debunk the pervasive myth that we cannot eracism in our lifetimes.* As early as June 2020, just one month after George Floyd's murder, we witnessed accelerated change from organizations, state governments and non-profit organizations. Simultaneously, decisions were made and implemented to expunge public spaces of stereotypical symbols that represented Black persons as inferior or "other." Aunt Jemima is no longer on the pancake box. Confederate statues that gave a nod to the Jim Crow era are being removed across the country and NASA headquarters was renamed for "Hidden Figures" scientist Mary W. Jackson. The Confederate Flag was removed from Nascar – Nascar! Imagine that! President Biden's cabinet became the most diverse in history. There is much more to be done in wealth acquisition, career opportunities, education,

to name a few, but these are indicators that we can overcome racial oppression and it doesn't have to take a century.

3. *To inspire those who deny that racism exists to search their hearts.* Our fates are linked and building relationships to assure equity for all is in our best interest. Taking a line from the movie, based on Alice Walker's novel, *The Color Purple*, spoken by Whoopi Goldberg's character, Celie, "Until you do right by us, everything you even think about is going to fail." Black people, in particular, must receive equitable treatment as citizens and residents of the USA. Understanding that we are still a largely segregated society, we cannot count on chance encounters at the coffee shop, book store, or school play. We need to intentionally make plans to interact. Without intentionality the status quo rules the day. Protests showing a rainbow of people marching together to end terror, abuse and violence against Black persons are a testament to how linked our fates are. Martin Luther King, Jr. said it best, "whatever impacts one directly, impacts all indirectly."

4. *To learn to love one another and to love learning about another.* Transformative dialogue is rooted and nurtured in love. It takes love to listen to another. Paul Tillich reminds us that "the first language of love is to listen." Love is a powerful force. It is the most endurable power in the world. When we use love as our weapon of warfare we have the power to produce astonishing results. Love can engender a revolution of transformation.

My experience reveals and research supports that the more we spend time together, develop friendships and familiarity, the more likely we will be able to relate to one another, empathize with life experiences and overcome racial injustice. Many of my friends and I can attest to the do-ability of maintaining healthy inter-racial and inter-religious friendships. Without the salve of relationship, racism will continue to lurk in the shadows, denying commonality, preventing opportunity and breaking spirits. The free exchange of communication can help us do something about that.

SIDEBAR: "Friendship with a member of another group can promote an affinity for that group as a whole."– Thomas Pettigrew, a psychology professor. Linda Tropp, associate professor at the University of Massachusetts, Amherst, found that a single friendship can have a ripple effect on attitudes. In the laboratory, she paired up people of different races to engage in friendship-building activities, such as sharing embarrassing moments and cooperation in Jenga, a game involving building blocks. Afterward, participants reported initiating more interracial contact. "When you forge close relationships across group boundaries," Tropp says, "you become invested in the friend and their group."

My Social Location

Before I delve into the concepts of transformative dialogue, allow me to share some biographical information about myself. I begin here because it is critically important for anyone facilitating transformative dialogues about race to be self-aware of their own cultural identity, values, and assumptions in order to understand the cultural identities of others. While we are more similar biologically, we are quite different culturally.

French sociologist Pierre Bourdieu captures the salient differences in his concept of *habitus.* Bourdieu's research revealed that all people groups have a deeply-seated, all-encompassing set of preferred tastes, smells, feelings, ways of communicating, preferred ways to deal with authority, power and relationships. Caught rather than taught, these preferences defy cognition making the articulation difficult as to why we do the things we do, like the things we like, worship the way we worship, work the way we work, decide the way we decide and communicate the way we communicate. Professor Bryan Stone compares a form of life to Bourdieu's description of habitus as "organizes and situates human practices, structure in our actions in ways that remain largely unconscious to us."

In the USA, race is one of several key influences to shape habitus. Given that habitus operates in ways that remain largely unconscious to us, what may seem like a trivial matter to an outsider of a particular culture is in fact loaded with deep meanings raising the stakes for those involved. Consequently, when we yuck another culture's yum, we can generate deep-seated offenses, causing a rift that may be difficult to overcome.

Taking the time to examine what was caught and how our values, perspectives and beliefs were shaped, enables insight into other cultures. Additionally, self-reflection provides a base of comparison from self-identities to social constructs and linked fates in this world house in which we find ourselves.

Forms of life are shaped by race, class, gender and ethnicity. While it is true that each individual is unique, we are also like those with whom we share cultural identity, moreover, we are like every other human being. In essence, we are like no one; we are like some people and we are like everyone in our basic human need for love, food and belonging.

To that end, I offer a window into my cultural background which informs my worldview.

Reflecting on my life's journey, on many occasions I was chosen to receive exposure and education outside of my densely-populated Boston neighborhood. With six (6) brothers, my sophisticated aunt wanted to ensure that I received training in posture and poise. She enrolled me in ballet classes at the local community center, The Robert Gould Shaw House. I eagerly attended those classes wearing my bright yellow bathing suit in place of the traditional black leotard, which we couldn't afford to buy. After a couple of lessons, the private instructor awarded me a full scholarship to receive private lessons at her posh studio on Newbury Street in Boston. Several years later I competed in a modeling competition at Boston City Hall and was awarded a scholarship by the famed Mildred Albert, Boston's First Lady of Fashion, to the Academie Moderne Finishing School on Beacon Street, among "high society." Further, throughout my education teachers engaged me in thought-provoking conversations, special opportunities to expand learning, small gatherings at their homes, and serious engagement about my thoughts regarding education in communities of color. With my later seminary education, I mark a few similarities that I share with the prophet Moses. Exposed to life and education in Pharoah's household, Moses was uniquely equipped to help his kin, the Hebrew people, and improve their quality of life. My life experiences and education have consistently taught me how to translate among and between my own community and to those outside of my community. I've had a lifetime of learning the value of dialogue.

Thus far, by the grace of God, I have traversed from being a teen mom to ordained American Baptist minister, pastor, diversity, equity and inclusion consultant, scholar, preacher, activist, executive coach, friend, business owner, sister, auntie, mom to two incredible adults, and grandmother to one grandson. My world view is additionally shaped by the fact that I am a Black female, born and raised in Boston by a single mom who divided her attention among my nine (9) siblings. All of my education occurred in Boston academic institutions: Girls' High School; Emmanuel College and Boston University School of Theology. Additionally, my education has been enhanced by travel to eleven (11) countries; thirty-two (32) states and two (2) USA territories.

From the time I began reading at the age of three (3), I have cherished words. Words were my toys, beating out dolls, Easy Bake Oven, Twister, and jigsaw puzzles. Reading the dictionary was a favorite past-time. I liked the way words sounded, how they were formed when pronounced. 'Czechoslovakia' was a favorite; a great word to say but not easy to work into a sentence. However, I do remember, how as a pre-teen I would tell anyone who would listen about my few known facts about that country.

I learned from the influential words of Julian of Norwich, WEB Dubois, Robert Frost, Langston Hughes, Countee Cullen, James Baldwin, Shirley Chisholm, Maya Angelou, Barbara Jordan, Delores Williams, Nikki Giovanni and, oh so many more, that I could steal away and pray; analyze from the lens of a double-consciousness; take time for reflection on winter nights; speak truth to power through prose; celebrate my heritage; find passion in the anger; make a seat at the table of authority; speak truth to power through prose; rise from humble circumstances; orate powerfully; lead from the bottom and deliver sweet inspiration.

My supermom, single-handedly raised us with a healthy dose of mother wit, hard work, independence and strict discipline. Conversations at home, among my nine (9) siblings and mom were animated, loud, competitive with a lot of cross talk. My siblings and I vied to be heard, some more successful than others.

My mom is a no-nonsense, plain-spoken woman, who does not like to say things twice. When I was about six (6) years old, three of my brothers and I were in a cab with my mom. The cab driver was rather ripe, and I said, once, "I smell something." No one responded. I said it again, "I smell something." Still silence. For the third time, "I smell..." – thwap! My mom slapped me in the mouth. "Shut your mouth," she whispered through clenched teeth. I learned the value of dialogue by its absence. In my world, you obeyed adults and did not debate, argue or challenge. Don't get me wrong, my mom was loving and caring. She was a person of action, more than a person of words.

Each of the women in my life, my mom, paternal and maternal grandmothers, demonstrated perseverance and faith in God. Ascending to the status of homeowner and breaking the cycle of poverty, my mom demonstrated how to defy statistical prognostications and become more than an overcomer.

My brothers and I spent most childhood summers visiting my grandparents in Portsmouth, VA. They owned a large garden and grew corn, cucumbers, tomatoes, lima beans and other vegetables. I have fond memories of us climbing the trees to eat

14

fresh blackberries; accompanying my grandmother to the farm and gathering fresh vegetables for us and neighbors.

Morning and night, my paternal grandmother would get on her arthritic knees and pray to the unseen God. I thought it was the strangest thing. Curiosity getting the best of me, I would climb out of my bed and press my ear against her closed bedroom door. There I would listen to her earnest prayers. Just as she finished, I would dart away without notice. Often, after "havin' her talk with Jesus", the next morning, she would declare, to no one in particular, but to everyone, that God had shared a mystery with her or told her about someone's personal need. "The Lord told me Miss Mary (fictional name) over yonder needs some food for her and her chil'ren." Many times she would pick fresh vegetables from the garden and deliver them to a neighbor's house, sometimes leaving them on the stoop, other times ringing the bell and praying with them. Strangers, who were often drunk, knew they could get a meal and conversation at Ms. Thrower's house. Accordingly, they would "happen to pass by", just about the time that Grandma would be in her metal rocking chair digesting the evening meal. A conversation would begin. Undoubtedly, I would be nearby and she would declare, "Cheryl, go fix Mr. Jim (fictional name) a plate – a *man-sized* plate – of food." She held a genuine respect for all.

In addition to Grandma's faith providing her intuitive insight into other's lives, she and Granddad built their home and helped each of their five children purchase land and build their homes. People were always visiting and conversations happening. Looking back, perhaps the summer trips were my early experiences with the power of dialogue. Grandma never lectured people about their drinking or circumstances. She listened and shared her perspective, wisdom and prayers. I noticed how people felt seen, heard and nourished by their interactions with her. Relationship building was happening right before my eyes.

My maternal grandmother migrated to NYC from the cotton fields of South Carolina at a young age. Upon her arrival, she was diagnosed with typhoid fever. After three months' stay at Bellevue Hospital in NY and nearly escaping death, she recovered and began work as a cook and domestic. She sacrificially lived on little and saved enough money to finance each one of her six siblings' transportation to the North. They called her Big Sister and we called her Big Mama. The nickname indicated more than her physical size. She laughed little, worked hard, read her Bible diligently and spoke when necessary. She was an advocate of *quid pro quo*. As a case in point, upon "giving" my oldest brother a bureau for his new apartment, she required that he pay ten dollars for the gift. When he objected, she explained that "if you don't pay nothin' for it, you won't think nothin' of it." I'll never forget that adage. It has stayed with me and I am reminded of how we place a higher value on the things in which we invest our time, talent or money.

Many life lessons are caught rather than taught and these maternal giants instilled three main life lessons in me: persist, (no matter how great the obstacle), live by faith, and wisely discern how to use your gifts. One lesson these admirable women did not teach is the art of transformative dialogue. No, these were women who showed their love in deeds rather than in words. Their responsibilities to provide for their families left little time for lengthy conversations.

Naturally, I admire what these ancestral women achieved against formidable odds. They paved the way for me to own a business, and to facilitate and lead dialogues in churches, synagogues, corporate, non-profit and community settings.

To become the beloved community, we must listen and learn to love one another, exploring, examining and exchanging ideas so that we can assure equity in the systemic patterns, structures, formal and informal practices and policies that govern our lives.

Christianity primarily informs my worldview and the role I believe I am called to play in the world. Putting the gospel into work-clothes for me, is by helping people to listen and learn our way to the beloved community through transformative dialogue.

What is Dialogue

"We have dialogue within us. Indigenous cultures, in particular know about dialogue."

Allyn Bradford, professor of dialogue

"Dialogue can enable people to engage in understanding and alter the cultural meanings present within society—to heal the sources of mass conflict and violence or ethnic bigotry."

Patrick De Mare, psychologist

"Listening is such a simple act. It requires us to be present, and that takes practice, but we don't have to do anything else. We don't have to advise, or coach, or sound wise. We just have to be willing to sit there and listen."

Margaret J. Wheatley

"Dialogue is a process in which there is a true turning to one another, and a full appreciation of another as a genuine being."

Martin Buber[iii]

Foundationally, love undergirds the discipline of dialogue. With Christ's love, love of self and love of others, we are able to experience dialogue participants as equals. Transformative dialogue is an act of faith, embracing uncertainty and ambiguity, while relying on the intangible and the invisible for understanding.

Dialogue is a special kind of conversation, derived from ancient times and modernized by the renowned quantum physicist, David Bohm. Bohm traces the roots of Dialogue to the Greek "dia" which means through and "logos" which means "meaning of the word." Dialogue is a flow of meaning through words. He asserted that dialogue would kindle a new mode of paying attention, to perceive – as they arose in conversation – the assumptions taken for granted, the polarization of opinions, the rules for acceptable and unacceptable conversation and the methods for managing differences.[iv]

Transformative dialogue welcomes dissent and rejects false agreement. "Nice-Nasty" never works in transformative dialogue. "Nice-Nasty" is that false agreement where someone smiles with their lips only and nods to avoid conflict. No, in transformative dialogue, controversy is met with civility and viewed as an opportunity for creative abrasion. As we rub opposing ideas together, the friction sparks a fresh perspective, embracing deeper, more nuanced insight for greater understanding.[v] In transformative dialogue, participants learn to fight lovingly, own their disagreement without diminishing freedom to be authentic. It's a beautiful thing.

The purpose of transformative dialogue is to create opportunities for people of different racial identities to talk about the complexities of race and to reach new understanding through substantive conversations. Love enables us to harness our egos and humbly come to terms with our own thinking process and unconscious bias. Too often in our society, one goes along to get along. Not so in transformative dialogue. Transformative dialogue is a disciplined conversation from which meaning evolves collectively through mutual understanding, and non-judgmental acceptance of diverse points of view. In dialogue, participants are not trying to persuade listeners to adopt their world views, nor does the notion of who's right or wrong come into question. Transformative dialogue is the search for meaning through diverse, rich perspectives of the group. Through understanding and being understood, we change. We gain insights while listening deeply to one another. And we help uncover the imbedded perspectives that are occluded by our own cultural blind spots.

Paulo Freire diagrams dialogue as two poles linked by a mutual trust and hope. I envision the illustration to depict dialogue as a combination of horizontal relationships with one another and vertical relationships with God.[vi]

Diagram of Dialogue:

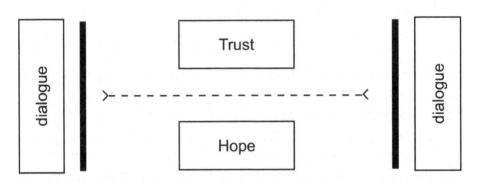

Those who engage in dialogue tend to be hopeful, trusting and reciprocal. They are able to balance silence and listening. They understand facts as they exist and do not seek to change them to fit a particular narrative or position. When we confront our own unconscious bias and gain new understanding, dialogue leads to additional actions not previously attempted. Dialogue is an action that leads to other actions, such as noticing and implementing systems of equity to replace systems of inequity. Dialogue is a tool to not only talk about racial injustice but to identify ways to overcome it.

Conversely, anti-dialogue involves horizontal relationships in competition with one another. "Anti-dialogue tends to be arrogant, hopeless, mistrustful, and not reciprocal; asymmetrical, and superior to facts and therefore free to understand them as it pleases."[vii]

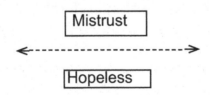

Please note the distinction I make between mistrust, which is based on instinct and a general lack of confidence, compared to distrust which is acquired through experience and is a more complete lack of trust. Mistrust has no foundation other than, perhaps, gut feel.

Uniquely created, humans have the ability and need to communicate.

Dialogue, which is essential to transformation, relies on reflection and action. Looking to the wisdom of Paulo Freire; *"Men and women cannot be truly human apart from communication; to impede communication is to reduce people to the status of things."*[viii]

Transformative dialogue is a counter-cultural response to our debate culture. Debate is the binary tool of conformity. Society relies on binary choices to maintain the status quo. Participants justify and defend assumptions by telling, selling and persuading in a competitive sharing of ideas to gain agreement. In debate you are either with the majority or minority, causing one to be an insider or outsider. Most of us prefer to be insiders which makes conformity the path of least resistance.

Conversely, transformative dialogue allows for the consideration, exploration and often, integration of multiple perspectives. Participants uncover and examine assumptions and develop shared meaning. Transformative dialogue never devolves into "whatabout-ism" nor is it a prescriptive model that focuses on a bottom-line result. Rather it is a process that allows open-endedness, welcomes surprises and makes space for learning.

The following chart is provided to help discern whether or not we are engaged in transformative dialogue rather than debate.

21

Transformative Dialogue vs. Debate[ix]

In TRANSFORMATIVE DIALOGUE, relationship is the priority	In DEBATE, winning is the priority
Relational – RB4T (relationship before task) seeks to connect, not alienate; shares power and leadership values the collective fosters a culture of cooperation	Competition – WB4R (win before relationship) seeks to convince, not collaborate; hoards power and leadership values individualism fosters a culture of zero sum
Holistic: two or more sides work together to create a fuller picture of reality – willingness to change perspectives	Finite: two or more sides oppose each other arguing a position to prove the other wrong
Deep listening and reflection; exploring own assumptions for re-evaluation	Inattentive listening; holding to own assumptions as truth
Enlarges a point of view improves thinking searches for strengths in others' thinking	Negating other party's perspective limits thinking searches for flaws in others' thinking
Suspends certainty, remaining open to previously unforeseen outcomes	Adheres to certainty, unwilling to consider alternative outcomes or perspectives

Transformative Dialogue is a conversation in which people think together in relationship and build upon existing strengths to achieve systemic racial equity. It requires participants to maintain a learning stance, shelve preconceived expectations and live in the realm of questions. Like a road with many curves and turns, participants are invited to travel until there is clarity. Open-ended questions are the glidepath to a reflective learning process that can lead to more informed actions for racial equity.

"What about this information is affirming/troubling to me?"

"Where have I seen this behavior in my life?"

"When have I been triggered in a similar way?"

"What racial barriers exist as a result of this practice/policy/ informal process?

"Given the systemic process who benefits? Who is disadvantaged?"

Open-ended questions, like those above, depart from the typical binary responses of agree/disagree; yes/no; right/ wrong; to deeper, more nuanced critical thinking. Living the questions has the potential of dismantling the status quo and deeply held, yet shallow beliefs. Maintaining a learning stance provides participants the opportunity to understand how systemic segregation from opportunity impacts BIPOC, while simultaneously shining a light on linked fates of all humanity. The Rev. Dr. Martin Luther King, Jr. emphasizes the reality of linked fates when he says; "Injustice anywhere is a threat to justice everywhere."

To practice the art of transformative dialogue requires a disciplined approach in how we speak and how we listen. This usually calls for a whole new set of conversation skills and habits and may result in a different and enriched attitude toward oneself and others.

In order for participants to have a R.E.A.L.© conversation, a Transformative Dialogue session must begin with a set of shared agreements. Some people call these ground rules or norms. I like to use the term agreements because it invites consent before proceeding. Do you agree to…?

I use the acronym R.E.A.L. © to formulate the agreements. A more expansive description of each term can be found in the workbook section on page xxx.

Respect...welcome input from others without judgment.

Engage... in self-exploration; uncover unconscious beliefs and assumptions.

Agree... to disagree – agreeably. Handle controversy with civility.

Lean.... into discomfort and listen, with curiosity, for surprises.

When leaders facilitate group dialogue, they must commit to listening without shaming or blaming. Instead of imposing their own point of view, facilitators need to give enough space for speakers to express themselves and learn what *they* think. At the same time, it is helpful for the facilitator to have a clear understanding of systemic implications to support a balanced and R.E.A.L.© conversation.

In the next chapter, I lay out some foundational concepts to build that base of information to truly support transformative dialogue.

"As individual stories emerge in the Dialogue process, these weave together like themes in music and create a shared meaning in a collective story, as in the epic tales of old." Allyn Bradford

Unblinding Eyes

As an aid to help unblind eyes that may not see the reality of the environment in which we exist, it is important for the transformative dialogue facilitator to have a solid foundation in some basic concepts.

"CAN'T-ITIS" (pronounced like arthritis)

Imagine the terrifying feeling of knowing that invisible systems are stacked against you. Despite being made in God's image, a diligent work ethic, steadfast academic achievements, consistent good will, simply because of the color of your skin, you are plagued with the disease of "can't-itis." You can't each your goals. You can't move into a neighborhood of your choice. You can't receive optimum health care. You can't attain the desired promotion. You can't receive acknowledgement of your education. You can't avoid the threat of incarceration, infant mortality, and on and on. All of this because an ideology is cemented into society that inhibits perception of your full humanity. The ideology does not only limit the full expression of BIPOC but of White people too. Because we are all in this life together.

"Can't-itis" is a condition that can be alleviated by first understanding the ideology that views Black people as inferior and White people as superior and then dismantling it so that it can no longer harm anyone. Here is one way the prevailing ideology plays out.

The **4 Is of Oppression** is commonly used to delineate how structural racism works. It is an interrelated system based on **ideas** and stereotypes. Beginning with an *ideology* or belief that Whites are superior to Blacks, *institutions* craft laws, policies, and practices that control others, ("Within incarcerated population, Blacks are overrepresented relative to percentage of the total population. African Americans comprise 13% of the population and represent 38% of the incarcerated population"[x] police excessive use of force, hiring policies, sub-prime loans), giving tacit permission for one group to *interpersonally* disrespect another with impunity (Blackface, racist jokes, stereotypes), all of this culminating in *internalization,* by members of the oppressed group, resulting in despair, powerlessness, and even violent aggression.

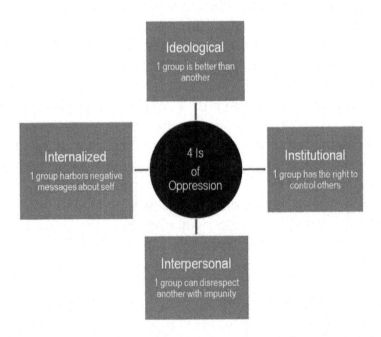

On the belief that racial disparities are the product, not of systems, but of individual behavior, the 4 Is prime people to search for the behavior of the individual rather than systemic injustice, institutional barriers and tacit permission for victimization. In fact,

Systemic Racism/Structural Racism/Institutional Racism are three different ways of referencing the complex interaction of policies, practices and culture that normalize and legitimize protection of unearned privileges for Whites while producing chronic disadvantages for Blacks in every major facet of life; housing, employment, education, health care, criminal justice and more. *White privilege is short-hand for those three different ways of referencing systemic racism.*

COLORBLINDNESS

"I have a dream that my four children **will** one day live in a nation where they **will not** be judged by the **color of their skin, but** by the **content of their character**".[xi] 8/28/1963 Rev. Dr. Martin Luther King, Jr. *I Have a Dream* speech.

"I don't see color;" is considered a compliment or a remedy to racism by those who tout colorblindness. But that's not what Dr. King had in mind when he used the phrase. **Colorblindness** supports the myth of meritocracy, guiding the misguided thinking that anyone can succeed – if they work hard enough. **Colorblindness** is the philosophy that race doesn't matter; a perspective which denies the existence of structural racism. Structural racism is predicated on the central premise that race matters. If a Black or Brown person is not succeeding, it's because: s/he is lazy; doesn't have the cognitive ability to make it; and/or doesn't speak the king's English. It's the person's fault and has nothing, whatsoever, to do with an ideology stacked against a person's success because of skin color.

If the problem resides in the person and not the system, then there's no need to implement intentional acts to correct past wrongs. Colorblindness asks the question, "What past wrongs?" Further, it carries the underlying message of "pull yourself up by your bootstraps", ignoring that no one gets ahead on individual effort alone.

The 4 Is of oppression reveal how much race does matter. As a matter of fact, race is embedded into every major facet of life.

According to 2018 US Census Data, the highest poverty rate by race is found among Native Americans (25.4%), followed by Blacks (20.8%), and Hispanics (of any race) at (17.6%). Whites and Asians both, had a poverty rate of 10.1%.[xii]

| 25.4% | 20.8% | 17.6% | 10.1% | 10.1% |
| Native American | Black | Hispanic | White | Asian |

ELECTED OFFICIALS[xiii] Of the 42,000 elected officials in the U.S.

- 90% of government officials are white
- 31% of our population control 65% of elected offices
- 71% of elected officials are men; 65% are White men

	WMen	WWmn	MOC	WOC
Elected Officials	61%	26%	8%	5%
Population	35%	37%	14%	14%

(WMen=White Men; WWmn= White Women; MOC=Men of Color; WOC=Women of Color)

UNCONSCIOUS BIAS

Unconscious bias is an auto-response, based on categorizations that our brains create with mental shortcuts to help us respond to the extraordinary amount of information we encounter on a daily basis. In the blink of an eye we react based on a narrative we've formed, often subconsciously.

Conversations about race are challenging, not only because of hostility, but largely because we are only 2% aware of our own biases.[xiv] The 98% that is beyond our consciousness makes us subject to the illusion of objectivity. Professor David Armor calls the illusion of objectivity, the notion that we are free of the very biases we're so quick to recognize in others.

When factoring in race, unconscious bias is prejudice in favor of, or against, a person, or group. It occurs instinctively and without one's awareness resulting in stereotypical reactions that can be positive or negative. © 2016

To summarize, structural racism does not require our awareness for it to work for or against us. The stealth bully or unseen belief system, like air, is always present affecting us all. If we do nothing, nothing changes. But if we take the time to acknowledge the system, dialogue about the impact of systemic racism, ah, then we have the opportunity to explore and determine what needs to change it and how to change it. Transformative dialogue can help us with that.

Robin DiAngelo suggests rather than asking the binary question; "is this or isn't this racist?"; a more honest question is "how does race factor into this situation?".

"Racism hurts (even kills) People of Color 24/7. Interrupting it is more important than my feelings, ego or self -image."[xv]
-Robin DiAngelo

Hold on to the concepts of systemic racism, colorblindness and unconscious bias, as we consider the value of dialogue in transforming the ideology of the 4 Is of oppression to an acknowledgement that we are people no more or less superior or inferior. Transformative dialogue can help us to listen and learn our way toward the beloved community.

Metaphors or visions of the center being held by one dominant group must be cast aside and replaced with what Jung Young Lee calls marginality. Centrality is solely hierarchical but marginality values interdependency and the wisdom of all as culminating leaders rather than a view held by a particular group. Marginality places everyone at the margin and negates any one person or group as central or the center.

SIDEBAR

"Dialogue is a process of genuine interaction through which human beings listen to each other with such depth and respect that they change based on what they learn."

(Cuentas and Linares Méndez, 2013). United Nations Development Program (UNDP)

Transformative Dialogue in Action

After the murder of George Floyd by a police officer in May 2020, a group of Attleboro residents, comprised of elected officials, district school administrators, clergy, and local organizations, decided to host a community dialogue on race. I had the privilege of designing the session. I also trained twenty (20) community residents to facilitate the dialogue about race and antiracism, none of whom had facilitated conversations on race previously. Our goal was to encourage attendees to non-defensively and non-judgmentally have a conversation about how racism impacts us all and the value of anti-racism. While we planned one dialogue, we hoped to generate an appetite for more group dialogues.

Titled *Neighbors in Dialogue: Listening and Learning from Each Other,* our online, inaugural event occurred on July 22, 2020. The response to our social media invitations was immediate. To our surprise and delight, more than 80 city residents registered within hours.

Our two-hour design was premised on education, information and conversation. The agenda included an overview, agreements, a brief video to assure common content, large group conversation in reaction to the video, then small-group, facilitated dialogues.

More than 85 participants showed up and remained for the entire session. After a short two hours, consciousness was raised. Witnessing the mixed-race audience share different perspectives about their racial experiences was inspiring. They revealed a shared understanding as they were guided to embrace controversy with civility and lean into discomfort without deflecting from the topic.

Participants expressed full-throated requests for more dialogues and publicly stated their stance on anti-racism in the closing portion of the session.

Some of the comments after the first dialogue:

"Once you see, you can't unsee."

"I used to think that it was enough not to be overtly racist. Now I realize that we must be actively anti-racist and break down the systems of white supremacy."

"I used to think I was open-minded and in tune about race. Now, I know I am complicit in white supremacy if I don't actively speak up. Speaking up doesn't come easily to me, but I'm going to do it."

"I used to think and feel that I had overcome my racism and now I know that it is a life-long process."

"I used to think I was not a racist, now I understand racism is systemic and I strive to be anti-racist."

"I used to think I was one of the only White people who was actively trying to become antiracist, and now I know lots of my neighbors feel the same way."

Neighbors in Dialogue continue to occur monthly, drawing more than 80 participants. At our ninth (9th) dialogue in July 2021, we compiled a community progress report and identified several positive outcomes for attendees, individually within the education system, our local political system and in local organizations.

In addition to the most obvious outcome of establishing meaningful dialogues among the most informed and those new to the topic of racism, participants reported; speaking out more against racism, encouraging their employers to actively stand against racism, advocating for hiring more people of color and noticing how mainstream media report racial identities of Black and Brown persons to the exclusion of the same reporting when White persons are involved. More frequently, attendees of Neighbors in Dialogue, notice how whiteness is centered as the norm. Participants recognized the absence of BIPOC at levels of authority in major industries as evidence of the need to decenter whiteness to make room for a more diverse representation of the USA population.

The superintendent, assistant superintendent, many educators, and staff members of the Attleboro School district participate as leaders and attendees of Neighbors in Dialogue. Several positive outcomes have occurred as a result of their participation, not the least of which includes: they have updated their hiring process to increase objectivity; and expanded recruiting sources to ensure a broader pool of candidates resulted in the hiring of a greater number of persons of color in teaching and administrative positions. The retributive student discipline process was replaced with a restorative approach to realize more racial parity among the student population.

Politically, some locally-elected officials are mentoring younger people of color who have expressed an interest in elected office, fostering opportunities for membership on commissions.

Some local non-profit organizations hosted dialogue sessions for their employee populations to foster a more inclusive and equitable work environment.

Now, in my Christian culture, we would say, "Won't God do it?! Hallelujah and Amen." Dialogue is our way of letting God in to "do it" with the power to transform people, processes and practices.

The entire facilitator training manual including the agenda for that first dialogue can be found in the workbook section on page 64.

WHAT MAKES CROSS-RACIAL DIALOGUE HARD?

While I tend to look at the glass half-full, I am a pragmatist. The work of fostering a beloved community is hard work and heart work. To craft a better future, we will need to risk vulnerability, broken hearts and perhaps risk learning that our deeply-held beliefs are at best, based on incomplete information and at worst, simply wrong.

I realize how painful it is for many BIPOC and understand how frightening it is for White persons to engage in dialogues about race and racism. Often, when I lead dialogues among mixed race participants, BIPOC are exhausted and traumatized by listening to White people examine, explore and share their experiences. They say things like:

> "What took White people so long to understand their role in perpetuating racism?"
>
> "I'm re-traumatized by these conversations; I just can't do it."
>
> From White people I hear:
>
> "I'm so uncomfortable; I don't want to say the wrong thing."
>
> "I feel so guilty about what BIPOC have gone through."

Here's the thing, too much blood has been shed. Too many tears cried and far too many opportunities lost to avoid the risk of pain and fear.

I feel great compassion both for the pain BIPOC experience to help White persons come to a shared understanding, and for White people who become paralyzed by guilt. Yet the dialogues are essential in taking all of us to a new place. Without the dialogues, the status quo prevails. Crafting a better future requires us to engage heart, soul, and mind; to comfort ourselves in the process and to face the fear and avoid paralysis. Heeding the words of Eleanor Roosevelt; "We must do the thing we think we cannot."

One aspect of human nature that makes transformative dialogue difficult is our desire to believe that we act free of prejudices and biases. David Armor defines the illusion of objectivity as the notion that we are free of the very biases we're so quick to recognize in others.

Conversations about race are challenging, not because of hostility, but largely because we are only 2% aware of our own biases. Well-meaning persons unwittingly allow unconscious thoughts and feelings to influence seemingly objective decisions. Research strongly suggests that no matter how well educated or personally committed to impartiality, most people harbor some unconscious or implicit biases. Without intentional work, the 98% remains beyond our consciousness.

Intentionality combined with self-compassion and compassion for others will go a long way in fostering productive, transformative dialogue. It is not unusual to be surprised and even hurt by our unconscious bias. But we can't beat ourselves up about it. Just as we extend kindness to others, we must do so for ourselves as well. It is good and right to acknowledge our embarrassment, hurt, disappointment. To deny those feelings delays our ability to grow from them. Psycholgists have learned that what we resist only grows stronger. So, don't resist the challenging feelings, embrace them, and allow them to guide your ability to mitigate the biases you do not want to harbor.

Another challenge to productive conversations about race is the lens through which we see the world. The authors of *A Many Colored Kingdom*[xvi] found:

> "Blacks and Whites view sources of racial tensions very differently, with Whites tending to look at the problems as individualistic and Blacks tending to see structural/ systemic issues as the primary source."

Further, research found Whites were particularly irritated when suggestions were made that anything other than individual responsibility was to blame for the plight of poor Blacks."[xvii]

Referring back to the tension between colorblindness and the 4 Is of oppression, another author, Emerson, states, "Whites seemed more irritated by the thought that inequities between Whites and Blacks might be due to structural/systemic issues than they were by the inequities themselves."[xviii]

When facilitating transformative dialogue, keep in mind that everyone comes to dialogues about race with their own theories about how society works, what methods will institute change and how they have been affected by race. The polarizing difference between Blacks along with most people of color groups who see events systemically, and Whites who see through the lens of individuality, requires deft listening and acknowledgement of the reality of both perspectives. Yes, there is plenty of data to support how racial injustice is structural. Simultaneously, there are numerous examples of individuals who have overcome structural barriers of injustice.

We must remember that a system is greater than the sum of the parts. Take, for example, the Stanford Prison Experiment that Professor Philip Zimbardo conducted in August, 1971. His aim was to study the effects of the institution on the behavior of individuals within its walls. Via a newspaper ad, he recruited volunteers and administered a battery of diagnostic and personality tests to eliminate anyone with psychological problems, medical disabilities, or a history of crime or drug abuse. Out of the 70 applicants, he selected 24 college students who he deemed to be normal, average, healthy middle-class males. Six (6) days into the fourteen (14) days study, he had to call it off. The abrupt ending occurred because of prisoners' pathological behavior and sadistic behavior by the guards. Regardless of how good the volunteers were, they fell victim to the institutional system of superiority and inferiority. Even though it was an experiment, the prisoners rebelled, broke down emotionally, and rejected group unity. The guards harassed, intimidated, humiliated and abused the prisoners. Some guards said they felt helpless to intervene, even though they did not agree with the treatment of the prisoners.

The Stanford Prison Experiment is a cautionary tale that can be applied to systemic inequity. Even if an individual is able to overcome systemic inequity, we cannot rely on individual victory extending to all in the system unless a systemic remedy is applied. As stated above, some of the guards noticed the problem but felt powerless to do anything about it. Transformative dialogue can help to highlight how structural injustice is the responsibility of all members of society.

Pew Research Center's 2019 report illustrates the vast difference in how Blacks and Whites perceive fairness. The divide gives an indication why dialogues about race can be emotionally charged. A commitment to be civil in the midst of controversy can minimize the tension and allow space to speak and to listen.

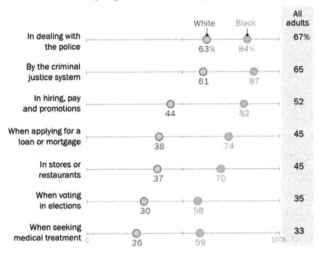

Whites and blacks differ widely in views of how blacks are treated

% of whites and blacks saying, in general in our country these days, blacks are treated less fairly than whites in each of the following situations

	White	Black	All adults
In dealing with the police	63%	84%	67%
By the criminal justice system	61	87	65
In hiring, pay and promotions	44	82	52
When applying for a loan or mortgage	38	74	45
In stores or restaurants	37	70	45
When voting in elections	30	58	35
When seeking medical treatment	26	59	33

Note: Whites and blacks include those who report being only one race and are non-Hispanic. "In dealing with the police" and "By the criminal justice system" were asked of separate random subsamples of respondents.
Source: Survey of U.S. adults conducted Jan. 22-Feb. 5, 2019.
"Race in America 2019"

PEW RESEARCH CENTER

Theologian Rev. Prathia Hall, proclaimed the gospel involved both the liberation of individuals and the redemption of systems for the benefit of all God's people. This "both/and" application is essential for us to overcome barriers to equity. In the next chapter, I explore how aversive racism works through individuals to perpetuate systems of inequity.

The Nature of Aversive Racism

The last challenge to productive dialogue that I want to mention is "aversive racism." This category of racist action is incredibly hard to pinpoint because it consists of a collection of subtle or cloaked behaviors and choices showing an aversion to interactions with persons of a different race. This aversive behavior is rarely explicit, and sometimes manifests unconsciously as ambivalence, apathy, or caution. In addition, it often presumes commonality of these aversions among other members of a person's own race.

Gaertner and Dovidio coined the term to convey their finding that "many Whites who consciously, explicitly, and sincerely support egalitarian values and genuinely aspire to be non-prejudiced, also harbor negative feelings and beliefs about Blacks and other disadvantaged groups."[xix] Because "aversive racists" harbor unconsciously negative feelings toward Blacks, the feelings get expressed in subtle, indirect and rationalizable ways.

"Discrimination will tend to occur in situations in which normative structure is weak, when the guidelines for appropriate behavior are vague, or when the basis for social judgment is ambiguous." In addition, discrimination will occur when an aversive racist can justify or rationalize a negative response on the basis of some factor other than race. Under these circumstances, aversive racists may engage in behaviors that ultimately harm Blacks but in ways that allow them to maintain their self-image as nonprejudiced.[xx]

Research shows that in the face of strong social norms, when discrimination would be obvious to others and themselves, "aversive racists" will not discriminate against Blacks." They will avoid feelings, beliefs and behaviors that could be associated with racist intent.

A prime example of aversive racism was provided when Las Vegas Raiders Coach Jon Gruden abruptly resigned in October, 2021. According to reporting by the New York Times, [xxi]Gruden wrote numerous emails to his inner circle and close colleagues in which he frequently used racist, homophobic and misogynistic language. Outside the earshot of the public, Gruden's communications, over a seven year period, indicate a culture of acceptance and tacit agreement among those with whom he communicated in the NFL and ESPN. Aversive racism flourishes in environments where guidelines for appropriate behavior are vague.

To further illustrate how aversive racism works, I offer the following fictional story.

Subtle forms of racism:

A middle-aged White male, we'll call him Ed, has a Latina daughter. As the White real estate agent was showing Ed a new home, Ed asked if the schools were integrated in the area. In hushed, conspiratorial tones the agent assured him that he didn't need to worry about mixed races in this white suburban community. Ed did not bother to tell the agent that he was the new pastor in the area and an advocate of social and racial justice. Nor did he share that he was the father of a Latina daughter. Ed simply concluded his meeting abruptly and did not return to the agent or that particular neighborhood

Aversive racism presumes solidarity based on racial similarity. In other words, the White realtor assumed the White buyer would share his views on segregation. In fact, Ed was seeking a neighborhood in which his family would be comfortable and welcomed. I'm certain you have your own examples of aversive racism and encourage you to think of ways you can counteract those presumptions.

One last thing, compassion and forgiveness are essential to generating the benefits of transformative dialogue. We must remember that it is possible for White persons to go from cradle to grave without ever having a substantive relationship with BIPOC. Likewise, few BIPOC can identify a meaningful relationship with White persons. With that reality, we all have a learning curve to arc. As we are listening and learning, we are bound to make mistakes, say the wrong thing, offer an inappropriate connection. When those moments occur, we need to exercise self-compassion, compassion toward others and forgiveness. Doing so will allow us to embrace a growth mindset and move on to producing the kind of transformative dialogue that will make a difference.

We've talked about what makes productive transformative dialogue challenging. In the next chapter, I explore three rules, beginning with the Golden Rule, to highlight cultural differences.

Golden, Platinum and Iridium Rules

"What does the Lord require of you but to do justice, and to love kindness, and to walk humbly with your God?" Micah 6:8

In a multiracial community, doing the work of justice requires us to understand the different perceptions of power from a cultural lens. Let's review power from the perspective of three rules; the Golden Rule, the Platinum Rule and the Iridium Rule.

The use and misuse of power can be clearly seen in communication styles. Euro-Americans tend to operate as if the English they speak does not need to be translated. Everyone else has to translate their language. African Americans speak English, however, because of their habitus, are often asked to translate what they say. If not asked to translate, often, a well-meaning, White colleague, might offer, "What she means is..." or "What he's trying to say is....." In order for these two indigenous groups to understand each other, they will need to recognize different is not deficient and translation is needed for both groups. The cultural differences, word choices, phrasing and perspectives from either group can be misinterpreted requiring both parties to take the time to translate to one another and assure understanding.

Translation isn't enough to ensure effective dialogue, one also must learn to notice the signs of power. Who talks most often? Who speaks first? Who is ignored? Whose ideas are acted upon? Whose comments are received as a joke?

In a situation in which a leader needs to elicit information from a group, in American society, the usual way is to simply ask people to volunteer the information. The practice is based on the universal belief that "we are all equal; therefore, if one has something to say, the person will say it." For participants with a strong sense of agency, that is, they understand and accept their individual power to assert their ideas and opinions, volunteering information is an accessible process. However, for participants who adhere to a hierarchical culture in which deference is given to the person in authority, they may not offer input unless specifically asked to do so. Theologian, Eric Law recommends, the practice of "mutual invitation." He suggests asking the person specifically for input, e.g., "Cheryl, would you like to offer your perspective?"

Power Rule #1: *The Golden Rule – "Do unto others as you would have them do unto you."* The widely known Golden Rule, found in Matthew 7:12 and Luke 6:31 is endorsed by all the great world religions.

> **Confucianism:** "Do not do to others what you do not want them to do to you" Analects 15:23

> **Hinduism:** "Listen to the essence of Dharma. Having listened, focus on it, and establish it in your mind. Do not do anything to others which you do not want to be done to yourself." Vedas

Judaism: "What is hateful to you, do not to your fellow man. This is the law: all the rest is commentary." Talmud, Shabbat 31a.[1]

The golden rule is a good rule that presumes homogeneity and sameness. In order for me to do unto others as I would have them do unto me, I must assume that the "other" appreciates what I appreciate; values what I value and considers important what I consider important. Now, some people certainly have similar values to mine, and also many people groups don't. So, yes, we need to abide by the Golden Rule and we need to augment it with our second rule of power.

Power Rule #2: *The Platinum Rule –* "*Do unto others as they would have you do unto them.*" Ahhh, now this rule considers difference and requires that we seek to understand others who hold values, beliefs, cultures, heroes and sheroes that are unfamiliar to us. The only way to do unto others as *they* would have us do unto them is to get to know something about the other. Together, *The Golden Rule and the Platinum Rule* expand our perspective from exclusive to inclusive of all people groups.

Do unto others as you would have them do unto you. Do unto others as they would have you do unto them.

But we can't stop there. I've created…

Power Rule #3: *The Iridium Rule –* "*Do unto others, with them, when they cannot do for themselves.*" I've coined this new rule because like the metal, it can be the densest and most corrosion-resistant rule when violated.

Iridium is the second densest element and the most corrosion-resistant metal known, even at temperatures as high as 2000 C. It is hard, brittle, and has the tenth-highest melting

---

[1] www.religoustolerance.org

point of all elements. Due to the combination of elasticity and rigidity, iridium has a high degree of stiffness and resistance to deformation. Iridium is virtually indestructible, even acid cannot attack the metal.

People can also become hard and brittle when things are done *for* them yet *without* them. Mahatma Ghandi was onto something when he said, "What you do for me, but without me, you do against me." All are free moral agents and individual agency must be acknowledged before swooping in to provide help.

However, there is one element that can attack and break down iridium – SALT. Salt has the power to break through iridium. "You are the salt of the earth; but if salt has lost its taste how can salt be restored?" (Matthew 5:13) We are placed here to be salt to bring out the God flavors of the earth. In this case, salt is respect – respecting that people are capable of taking care of some of their own needs. The iridium rule respects that a helicopter parent is not needed to fend off, deflect or provide the help that doesn't help. People, particularly BIPOC, are capable of performing at a high level, addressing needs and responding to issues. The iridium rule acknowledges BIPOC's individual agency and embraces dialogue as a common denominator for understanding at an individual level to fuel action at a systemic level.

When insiders dysfunctionally rescue, they leap in to help before clarifying any actual need. They send a message that the rescued cannot function without the rescuer. When the bi-lingual/ multi-lingual person struggles to complete a sentence and the listener leaps in to finish the sentence for the speaker, the listener conveys that either the speaker is incapable of communicating verbally or that the listener has no time to wait for the speaker to complete their thought. Either way, the impact is disrespect. When we consider whole populations of people as inferior, the impact is disrespect. Societal barriers based on arbitrary differences are corrosive and destructive. We can break down the barriers, the dysfunctional, disrespectful behavior that society dictates by engaging in the counter-cultural characteristic of honoring individual power and exercising the Iridium rule.

The Iridium rule deepens the level of respect for the "other" by acknowledging that other people have gifts and talents that are helpful to communities and society at large. The iridium rule helps us to avoid dysfunctional rescuing, to recognize different approaches, methods and processes that may be different from our own, but still attain a desired goal. However, if we leap in to rescue the "other" by doing for the "other" what the "other" can do for themselves, we are not only disrespectful, but also disempowering, disengaging and destructive. It weakens the other.

The Golden Rule, Platinum Rule and Iridium Rule each operate as a collective to allow for building relationships across difference. These three power rules provide a helpful framework for engaging in productive dialogue that relies on a stance of inquiry and advocacy.

Golden Rule: "Do unto others as you would have them do unto you."

Self-reflection is a pre-requisite for abiding by the Golden Rule. You must have an understanding of how you want to be treated. Some questions to prompt you include: What gives you life/energy? What detracts from life/energy? What is your preferred communication style? How do you want to be listened to? What is your relationship to time? When you feel most respected, what is happening?

Platinum Rule: "Do unto others as they would have you do unto them."

Getting to know others is a pre-requisite for abiding by the Platinum Rule. The words of Stephen Covey, "Seek first to understand before seeking to be understood", resonate with the Platinum Rule. What do you understand the other party to prefer? What evidence do you have for your conclusion? What do you notice from the other party's behavior? Are they silent with you and animated with others? How much time are you willing to dedicate to the goal of learning more about those who are different from you? Are you vulnerable and transparent or guarded?

Iridium Rule: "Do unto others, with them, when they cannot do for themselves."

The *Iridium Rule* requires that you suspend certainty, act humbly and maintain a learning stance. An illusion of superiority persuades one to believe they know best, have the most relevant information, can implement the optimum solution, and therefore can be the most helpful. A superiority mindset believes that the best way to help is to intervene, but like the process of transitioning from a caterpillar to a butterfly, intervention to help can be fatal or debilitating. The butterfly must flap their wings to emerge from the chrysalis. Without struggle, formation will not occur properly. Helping too soon is the help that doesn't help.

A Butterfly Fable

Imagine that you are intrigued with the transition process of the butterfly. You come across a chrysalis and notice movement. You devote some time to observing the process of the butterfly making its way to emergence, but it's taking longer than you anticipated. Then you notice a small hole and the butterfly is working to enlarge it to emerge. You get excited, it's about to happen! But the process is taking a long time. You think the butterfly is needlessly struggling so you decide to help. You widen the hole to make it easier for the butterfly to fly. With great pride, you wait. Instead of flying, the butterfly crawls out. The wings are soggy, soft and unformed. Flying is impossible. The butterfly is doomed.

You had such good intentions. How could your compassionate actions have created such a tragic result?

The process of eclosis takes anywhere from minutes to a couple of hours. In this case the butterfly needed to struggle through the process for the wings to develop correctly. Circumventing the process impeded that necessary step. Your help didn't help.

The fact that progress was not evident didn't mean progress was not occurring. The Iridium rule prevents a similar mistake by requiring interaction and engagement with the other party before leaping in with well-intended, yet misguided help.

Sidebar: Examples of violation of the iridium rule: finishing others' sentences; leaping into help before clarifying that there is an actual need; doing to someone rather than with someone, suggesting a lowering of aspirations to avoid disappointment or financial hardship; avoiding communication of constructive feedback for fear of being labeled an "...ist", or accusing one of throwing out the race card when they are describing an offense.

Exercising the three power rules helps us interact respectfully, humbly and equitably. Doing so reinforces shared power and acknowledges mutuality. None are inferior or superior.

The Church Universal

"For us, the church, there is only this task: to believe, and then turn to the work of removing chains from hearts, minds, spirits and bodies – chains that have already been broken."   (adapted) The Rev. Prathia Hall[xxii]

Clearly, brokenness is not God's intention. In God's divinity, God created diversity which requires active engagement of those standing in the gap to mend broken relationships and broken connection. The role of God's gapstanders – not bystanders or upstanders – is to love people enough to lead and engage in transformative dialogue to establish a new, inclusive, harmonious, heterogeneous counter culture for all of society to emulate.

I am frequently the only Black female in boardrooms; some denominational meetings and clergy settings. Across all of those, organizations are more willing to embrace racial diversity than the church, and that is sad to see. For organizations a self-preservation element is at play. Demographic changes determine that more people of color will comprise the US workforce, making for a sound business decision to embrace diversity. Nonetheless, my experience reveals that corporate leaders have a deep-seated desire to overcome the hurdle of anti-Black sentiment. "I don't know what to do." "Tell me how to change the work culture." "How can I get my Board to buy into increasing diversity as a business imperative?" "I volunteer with organizations committed to closing the racial gap, how can I bring those values into the workplace?"

In desperation they seek a practical way to sustain a fair and equitable work environment.

On the other hand, the church rarely expresses a desire to combat racial injustice. Too often I hear challenges to the realities of racism: "It's a social issue not for the church to undertake", "It's complicated" – as if complexity alone is enough to cause one to back off. "Why are we talking about race, there are other important issues the church needs to look at." "Conversations about race make people uncomfortable." "We don't need to focus on race, just follow Jesus." "Are you calling me racist?!" "I'm not racist." "People of color are not treated differently than Whites."

As a Christian, it pains me to see how so many American churches are still divided along racial lines. Ignoring racial injustice is antithetical to the work of Christ. God loves diversity and I imagine God weeps when witnessing how long the church is taking to transition from uniracial to thriving multiracial congregations.

Even before the prolonged street protests against systemic injustice, lay organizations were ahead of churches in intent and implementation of diversity. After May 2020, organizations moved at breakneck speed to effect change, diversify boards of directors; remove racist symbols and invest in Black businesses and social justice efforts. The faith community is being outpaced in becoming more diverse and inclusive. Perhaps partnerships with the faith community, progressive organizations and community leaders could improve traction toward the goal of overcoming systemic racial inequities.

Many church growth books advocate the *homogenous unit principle* as a strategy. The premise of that principle is that sameness breeds growth, efficiency and fulfillment. Author Michael Emerson[xxiii] conducted extensive research comparing the racial attitudes of Whites and Blacks in homogenous and in heterogenous congregations. His findings revealed that those in multiracial congregations are less likely to be upset if their children marry someone of another race; if their neighborhood is 75% their own race and 25% of other racial groups; or if time is dedicated to talking about racial issues. Although Emerson later realized that in multiracial congregations religious life is separated along racial lines, and members are more likely to have same race friendships resulting in fewer opportunities for cross-racial relationships and connections.[xxiv] The potential for the church to be a catalyst in cultivating a more equitable, racially just society is present, but requires breakthrough methods to overcome the hurdle that intergroup relationships are too difficult.

Emerson asserts that "we can predict that conflict will be most frequent and severe in multiracial congregations that contain people of both Black and White indigenous American cultures."[xxv] Both people groups believe they have an equal right to practice their culture and have little interest in giving it up. Therefore, in our polarized culture that rewards choosing sides, a multiracial congregation comprised of two American indigenous groups will have an impasse that results in at least a "twoness"--two worship services, two types of music, and two ways of decision making. Consequently, instead of a harmonious whole, what should be one becomes two halves which are not conducive to building relationships, community or equity.

When faith communities are divided along racial lines, the numerical majority receives tacit approval to perpetuate divisions based on race. After all, if the church, the beloved community, cannot operate in harmony, society cannot be expected to do better than the moral leader. The prophetic writings of noted author, W.E.B. DuBois ring true today, "...for the problem of the 20th Century is the problem of the color line."[xxvi] Further, what DuBois said when referring to the "Negro" can be said also of the church.

"It is a peculiar sensation, this double-consciousness, this sense of always looking at one's self through the eyes of others, of measuring one's soul by the tape of a world that looks on in amused contempt and pity. One ever feels his two-ness,—an American, a Negro; two souls, two thoughts, two unreconciled strivings; two warring ideals in one dark body, whose dogged strength alone keeps it from being torn asunder."[xxvii]

The double consciousness of which Dubois speaks, which extends into the current 21st Century, requires that outsiders become aware of the norms of other societies but with no responsibility for insiders to become aware of outsiders. Thus, BIPOC must be bi-lingual, that is, speak in the tone, style and cadence of White persons and speak in the cultural norms of their own culture. In other words, there is a coded language that determines whether one is taken seriously, and heard. The impact of these types of encounters hits the pocketbook, job opportunities, housing, etc. Sadly, even if one masters the coded language, the darker hue is still a barrier to achieving an equal quality of life as White persons. Consequently, relationships must be formed that extend beyond opportunities. Even into the 21st Century, White persons can go from cradle to grave without forging a meaningful relationship with a BIPOC. Pursuing relationships outside of one's racial identity is a choice that insiders are privileged to make.

I once heard someone say that the church is a movement, not a monument. Bricks and mortar do not define the church, instead it is a people who are renewed daily and transformed by interaction with one another and the incarnational presence of God for the purpose of manifesting the beloved society.

To nurture the movement, we must notice when we are behaving in ways that yield a zero-sum result. When we celebrate our habitus to the denigration of another, we are denying the possibility of co-existing. It is in the jokes that we laugh at when in our homogenous group settings, or the askew glances that our authority figures deliver to what is perceived as wayward behavior, or the repeated comments about the bright colors, subdued colors, loud talking, whispers, word choices, length of service, who should be in charge, etc. The perceived innocence of "what is that smell?" or "what are you eating?" could signal a message of not belonging. A rejection of musical selections, cadence in prayer, length of worship service, all have to be worked out respectfully with an understanding that different is not deficient. Influences are also seen in how Blacks and Whites perceive space, time, worship styles, resources, leadership styles, hierarchy, identity, and power.

We can no longer accept a "nice-nasty" attitude: that is the smile on one's face and scowl behind the other's back that happens when beliefs defy behavior. Disingenuousness must be replaced with sincere action to be inclusive. Behaviors must extend beyond Sunday and become a part of policies, practices and norms in institutions, education, housing and employment and social interactions.

The Church must begin to ask, "Why would that ever be okay with a loving, inclusive God? Why would it ever be okay to block opportunities because one is of a different race? Why would it ever be okay to provide a substandard level of healthcare because one's zip code is not in an affluent community? Why would it ever be okay to reject one because of their gender or gender identity? Why would it ever be okay...?

In other words, we can't say "yes, the church is for everyone," and then go into society and actively engage in racially unjust behavior. To do nothing maintains the status quo. To operate at an individual level perpetuates the status quo. To assuage the turmoil and tap into what is inherent in indigenous peoples, the ability to engage in transformative dialogue; to embrace it and to welcome the transformative power of the Creator to speak through creation, will not only change participants but ultimately neighborhoods, communities and society at large.

The urgency of now is upon us and we must build on the momentum that is in the atmosphere for the beloved community to spread. In this book, you will find theories, frameworks, and tools for both the church and organizations to courageously facilitate transformative dialogues.

Our purpose is learning and listening our way toward the beloved community. May the ensuing conversations, in Christ's Spirit, be transformative.

Sidebar: "burr is a seed or dry fruit in which the seeds bear hooks or teeth which attach themselves to fur or clothing of passing animals or people. The hooks or teeth can be irritants and very hard to get off of clothing, such as wool or cotton. It was the inspiration for Velcro."

The burrs of tradition are so difficult to remove from our cultural mapping that we unconsciously view others' church traditions as wrong, weird or as anti-worship. Many traditions get us into the "It's not church without...." For example:

"It's not the church... without formality; i.e. referring to people by putting a handle on their name, such as, Reverend, Deacon, Sister, Mother, Ms. Mr. etc. or

"It's not the church... without informality; i.e. referring to people by their first names rather than title; shortening a name, even if the person introduces themselves using their full name -e.g. Bob for Robert, Liz for Elizabeth, etc.

Faith communities are well-intentioned to build relationships, share power and to nurture communities of respect, but for all of the reasons stated above, too frequently have an opposite impact.

Considering the amount of information that we must distill on a daily basis in this information age, understandably we rely on categories and labels as shortcuts to identify one another. However, the shortcuts we typically impose often become stereotypes by which we label others. Frequently our shortcut labels are based on social constructs and groupthink rather than observed or known characteristics. That's the work of God's gapstanders: to discern where the disconnects are and work interdependently to fill the gaps with expanded knowledge and increased understanding. Habitus affects the dynamics of spiritual formation based on the combined experiences of the church community.

A material culture needs something to hang on to. The material culture, while not bricks and mortar, can be just as visible by way of a new tradition, new habitus, new infrastructure, new kinds of burrs. Hooks and teeth aren't all bad; the presence of definable processes, reliable structures, and trustworthy rhythms that can be relied on and trusted can provide the platform for a new spiritual formation. The formation is developed through social connections, Bible studies, preaching, and other shared activities. It is established, meal by meal; agreement by agreement; meeting by meeting; word by word: precept by precept; dialogue by dialogue.

Four dominant frames of race-related issues[xxviii]

To nurture multi-racial communities and to remove obstacles to spiritual formation, it would behoove church communities to dialogue about distinctly different perspectives on space allocation and usage, time orientation, leadership, and resources.

SPACE

Regarding space, some of the questions that multiracial churches will need to devote time to dialoguing: how the building and facilities are used; when the building and facilities will be used and by whom; and how decisions will be made for space utilization. Another significant question for multiracial communities is where certain events can occur. For example, can the sanctuary be used for anything other than structured worship services? Many of the predominately Black churches in my experience have a sacrosanct attitude about the sanctuary and its furnishings. For instance, strict rules about not eating in the sanctuary, or not touching or putting anything on the communion table. Granted this is not every predominately Black church but many hold a reverent view of the worship space and the furnishings. Conversely, in many predominately White churches that I've attended, there is a more relaxed view of the worship space. As a case in point, in the churches that I've attended with movable pews, the sanctuary has been converted into a theater for plays, a concert hall and a dining hall. Fewer rules existed about what could be touched or moved.

TIME IS A CULTURAL PHENOMENON

The topic of time is significant in a multiracial community. Different cultures value time differently. Understanding that people groups are either time-oriented or event-oriented can go a long way toward understanding how to engage in transformative dialogue for mutual coexistence and spiritual development. Lingenfelter and Mayer[xxix][2] offer an accessible chart to scope out the differences between the two concepts of time.

2

Time Orientation	Event Orientation
1. Concern for punctuality and amount of time expended	Concern for details of the event, and people attending, regardless of time required
2. Time is fixed, sacred; to be late is rude	Time is fluid, flexible, imprecise; to be late is life
3. Prioritizes tasks and principles	Prioritizes persons and relationships
4. Careful allocation of time to achieve the maximum within set limits	Exhaustive consideration of a problem until resolved
5. Tightly scheduled, goal-directed activities	A "let come what may" outlook not tied to any precise schedule
6. Rewards offered as incentives for efficient use of time	Stress on completing the event as a reward in itself
7. Emphasis on dates and history	Emphasis on present experience rather than the past or future
8. Finds satisfaction in the achievement of goals	Finds satisfaction in interaction
9. Accepts loneliness and social deprivation for the sake of personal achievements	Deplores loneliness; sacrifices personal achievements for group interaction

As the chart illustrates, people who are time-oriented value punctuality, precise starting and ending times and getting the most out of the time used. On the other hand, people who are event-oriented place a high value on spontaneity, a less structured process and task completion rather than the length of time it takes to finish a project. While time-oriented persons organize their day into specifically planned time periods, event-oriented persons have a general idea about their schedules and maintain a flexibility to go with the flow. Many event-oriented persons do not wear a watch while time-oriented persons cannot imagine leaving the house without their timepiece. Event-oriented persons may view time-oriented persons as overscheduled, uptight, and tense. Conversely, time-oriented persons may view event-oriented persons as disorganized, lazy and laid back.

On average, a higher percentage of Black persons and persons of color are event-oriented while a higher percentage of White persons are time-oriented. Multiracial communities will need to engage in transformative dialogue around a mutually collaborative worship experience. How will the faith community meet the needs of the different time preferences without subjugating either? When will worship begin? If worship starts at a precise time, will there be flexibility for a portion of the service to be more spontaneous and less structured?

LEADERSHIP

Since Black people's cultural orientation tends to be hierarchical, the view of leadership is highly regarded. Thus the pastor is seen as the primary authority figure. Correspondingly, the sermon is central in the worship service. Conversely, White people's cultural orientation tends to be distributed authority, which lends itself to seeing the pastor as an employee of the church with no more authority than any other church member.

RESOURCES

Because of historical patterns of inequity in U.S. society, Whites more often have more resources, financially and otherwise, than Blacks. Correspondingly, those who have the most resources can usually be found in decision-making roles. In order for multiracial congregations to thrive, we need to de-couple resources from leadership. Simply because an individual or group has more does not mean they are best suited for leadership. In an equitable multi-racial congregation, financial clout cannot be the main priority of leadership.

Bridging the Unbridgable

"As race was seen as determined by biology, the differences between the white people and their counterparts were considered unchangeable and unbridgeable."[xxx]

"Good fences make good neighbors" [xxxi]

How does Robert Frost's American proverb compare to Jesus' instruction "to love your neighbor as yourself?" [xxxii]

Yale University's ivy fence established the illusion of separation and safety from the city environs of New Haven. Until February 17, 1991, the administration, faculty and students were not disabused of the formidable strength of their fence. On that fateful day, the Yale community's confidence in the ivy barricade was shattered. Christian Haley Prince, a fourth generation, 19-year-old white male undergrad at the prestigious ivy league school, was allegedly shot and killed by James Duncan Fleming, a 16-year- old Black male student from the New Haven school of hard knocks. After 2 trials, Fleming was acquitted of Prince's murder. No longer could the Ivy League be shielded from the shared experience of being a neighbor in the New Haven community; the chasm between poverty and privilege, pigment and prospect fused linking two divergent worlds of the haves and have nots. Two adolescents tragically became casualties of the systemic belief that rigid boundaries can remain in a malleable society. No longer could Yale neglect the needs of the city. Yale could certainly not ignore the system of inequity, and poverty. The administrators recognized the communal benefit of partnering with New Haven to create, via relationship, rather than fences, a safer environment for students, faculty and residents.

In 1995, Yale President, Richard Levin created the Office of New Haven and State Affairs (ONHSA). It is now called Office of New Haven Affairs.[xxxiii]

"Yale University has called New Haven home for three centuries and the future of the university is inextricably tied to the strength of our hometown."[xxxiv]

Yale partners with its neighbors to strengthen New Haven through fostering economic development, revitalizing neighborhoods, supporting public school and youth programs and creating a vital downtown.

Jesus' geographical metaphor is not familial (e.g. "mother" or "sister") nor ethnic (e.g., "your people"). It admonishes us to spend time with, not wall off from our neighbors.

We now recognize that race is a social fabrication. According to a 2018 study by Northwestern University and 23andMe, science shows "genetic differences are not significant enough to support biological definitions of racial categories. While genetic variations reflect different ancestral groups, any two individuals are 99.5 percent genetically similar." In other words, race is a myth while racism is real.

Despite the genetic similarity, skin color radically influences outcomes inclusive of health, criminal justice, unemployment, and early education. Black people fare much worse compared to Whites, regardless of the state in which they live.

Just as my grandmother testified of God unfolding mysteries to her in her prayer closet, God continues to reveal answers to God's gapstanders to help repair humanity's brokenness. Gapstanders are the courageous individuals who implement counter-cultural methods, like transformative dialogue to usher in the beloved community. The pollution of racism permeates all aspects of our lives. In recognition of systemic racism's impact in housing, criminal justice, wealth, and racial disparities, the Biden/Harris Administration took a step in the right direction and rolled out a series of executive orders placing racial equity at the whole of government.

A wide array of data supports the need for addressing systemic racism. Eliminating racism will not result in transference of disparities for White persons. Embracing a mindset of abundance instead of scarcity can help us all see that enhancing the quality of life for BIPOC helps everyone. Transformative dialogue helps us see the mutual engagement of the whole is needed to gain a larger, more comprehensive view. Making room for all means greater creativity and opportunities for more ways to expand equity for all. Without limitations the beloved community can unfold in untold and pleasantly surprising ways. Transformative dialogues across race require courage, faith, perseverance and hope – lots of hope.

"The intention of dialogue is to reach new understanding and, in doing so, to form a totally new basis from which to think and act. We do not merely try to reach agreement but we try to create a context from which many new agreements might come. And we seek to uncover a base of shared meaning that can greatly help coordinate and align our actions with our values." [xxxv]

A New habitus

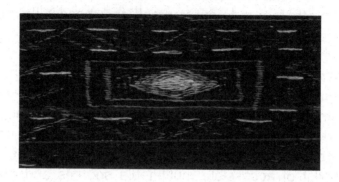

How sweet it would be if a new habitus were undertaken by leaders throughout the country by helping mixed-race, multi-gender groups have meaningful conversations about race and unity. With an aim to build on the beautiful diversity of humanity and the sincere curiosity to learn more about one another, we could take space for our own perspectives and make space for others. Now, don't misunderstand me, I'm not referring to assimilation or a melting pot. Instead, the metaphor of an intricate tapestry better illustrates the new habitus. Made in a variety of hues and shapes, the tapestry represents distinction and unity, variety within individuality and coexistence without diminishment. Each part of the tapestry making a significant contribution to the whole without loss of value. Each part taking the space it needs to add value to the whole.

Before introducing the next section of practical tools for application, allow me to say some concluding remarks. This work; the work of deeply listening to one another is taxing. It can be discouraging when some people are at the beginning of the learning curve on race. This work must be infused with joy, compassion, forgiveness, love and laughter. If you don't find moments to laugh throughout doing this work, maybe you don't need to be involved in it. A healthy sense of humor will make the difference. Search for the moments to laugh at yourself, to laugh with others and to cut yourself and those with whom you dialogue some slack.

A companion workbook is available, *"The Divinity, Diversity & Dialogue Workbook: Practical Resources to help Facilitate Transformative Racial Dialogues."* It includes accessible frameworks, stories, and exercises to provide a head, heart and hands approach to aid in facilitation and engagement. You will find a toolkit of accessible multimedia sources and articles to enhance understanding, practice new learning and implement dialogue events to promote inclusion and equity.

Thank you for your leadership in guiding neighbors into the beloved community through listening and learning. Eracism and expanding the beloved community through dialogue is a process. It is happening, as evidenced by our experience in Attleboro, MA. With your time, talent and investment it will happen in your community and we can exponentially expand the terrain of the beloved community.

End

Neighbors in Dialogue Facilitation Guide

To provide some practical applications for engaging in productive dialogues regarding race, I am providing a copy of the guidebook I created to train facilitators for "Neighbors in Dialogue" sessions in Attleboro, MA. In addition, there are a few frameworks to help facilitators get started.

To encourage you in this work, please remember, we began having "Neighbors in Dialogue" sessions in Attleboro in July 2020, and the conversations continue. Some outcomes from the nine (9) sessions from 2020 to 2021, include;

- increased representation in community events
- a couple of regular dialogue participants returned to college to complete their education
- one community member became a high school educator
- others have received career opportunities, exposure and collaboration with local elected officials and
- many from education are making systemic changes in the local school system.

cheryl harris & associates, inc.
authentic :: purposeful :: effective

Facilitator Training Guide
For
Neighbors in Dialogue: Listening to and Learning from Each Other
The Reverend Cheryl Harris, M.Div.

The first language of love is to **listen**." Paul Tillich
Date: July 6 2020
Time: 6:00pm – 8:00pm

Zoom Meeting Link:

Prior to July 6 2020 training, please complete the following tasks:

1. **Read:** Reynolds, Jason and Kendi, Ibram X. *Stamped: Antiracism, Racism and You*

2. **Watch two videos:** Racism in America: American Psychological Association (20 minutes). https://www.youtube.com/redirect?q=http%3A%2F%2Fwww.apa.org%2Feducation%2Fundergrad%2Fdiversity%2Fdefault.aspx&event=video_description&redir_token=9VkbaAl-BuGm_mt6cPKtNLNtH-Z8MTU2NDA5NDY0NEAxNTY0MDA4MjQ0&v=6wjG4pQp1Zc

  a. Description: Scholars share a comprehensive view of the mental, physical, emotional and spiritual impact of racism

3. *__The danger of a single story__*, TED Talk by Chimamanda Adiche, offers insight to the phenomenon of using small bits of information to imagine who a person is. (18 minutes)

We began the workshop with a silent viewing of the images in Nelson's cover, followed by discussion of what emerged as the images were displayed.

https://www.newyorker.com/culture/cover-story/cover-story-2020-06-22

Description: Nelson, Kadir "Say Their Names"

A cover in which the murder of George Floyd embodies the history of violence inflicted upon Black people in America.

CONTENTS OF THIS TRAINING GUIDE

Page	Topic
3	Preparation for Training
4	Agenda for July 22nd
6	Illusion of Objectivity
7	Transformative Dialogue
8	Fundamental Concepts
11	Establishing a Positive Atmosphere & Facilitator Role
13	What Happens in Breakout Rooms
16	Key Facilitation Skills
17	Managing Participants and Questions

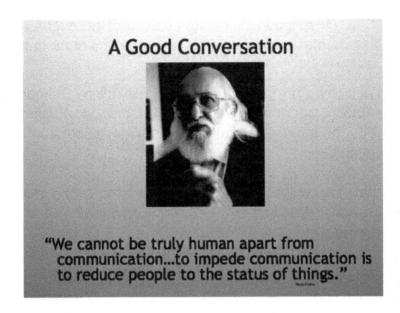

AGENDA for July 22, 2020

Purpose of Session: In this initial dialogue, we seek to listen and learn from the wisdom of individuals and the collective wisdom of the group. It will be a facilitated dialogue on Zoom that will involve large group and small group breakout sessions. In the two-hour period we will hear from our neighbors and explore the implications of racism and anti-racism.

Activity	Who	Time
Zoom Protocols		6:02-6:05
Welcome – establish inclusive atmosphere		6:02-6:05
Introduction – how we got here and sponsors		6:05-6:10
Overview & Centering Exercise		6:10-6:15
Set Expectations – "We have more questions than answers. It is a vast topic and we are just at the beginning. We are interested to know if you would like more conversations like this in the future. We would like your response at the end of this session.		6:15-6:18
Small group – breakout questions – all facilitators get same questions		
1. "When was first time you became aware of your race? Please share your story or experience."		
2. "In what ways have you noticed that race matters in society?"		
3. "What is the distinction between non-racist and anti-racist?"		6:25-7:30
LARGE GROUP SHARING – ask a question that captures what participants experienced, felt, or how thinking changed. Sentence stem "I was feeling/thinking this-now I feel/think that"		7:30-7:50
"I Too" Langston Hughes Read twice	By two different readers	7:50-7:55
Survey & Close		7:55-8:00

FUTURE: Anticipating that people will want more outlets to talk, we plan to have more conversations on this topic. If there is interest, we could plan for a facilitated series of 5-6 conversations, concluding with a community anti-racism project.

ILLUSION OF OBJECTIVITY

This is a moment of incredible consequence for our country. On streets across this nation, we are reckoning with generations of racism, oppression, and injustice. Dialogues, between White, Black and all persons of color, about racism and anti-racism are much needed.

Conversations about race are challenging, not because of hostility, but largely because we are only 2% aware of our own biases. (John A. Powell) The 98% that is beyond our consciousness makes us subject to the illusion of objectivity. David Armor calls the illusion of objectivity, the notion that we are free of the very biases we're so quick to recognize in others. Everyone comes to dialogues about race with their own theories about how systems of opportunity work, whether change can be negotiated or must be forced, to what extent people and institutions can be trusted, and how race and racism have impacted their lives.

The Pew Research Center's 2019 report illustrates the vast difference in how Blacks and Whites perceive fairness. The divide gives an indication why dialogues about race can be emotionally charged.

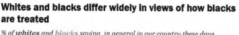

Whites and blacks differ widely in views of how blacks are treated

% of whites and blacks saying, in general in our country these days, blacks are treated less fairly than whites in each of the following situations

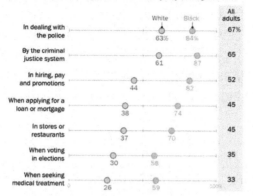

Note: Whites and blacks include those who report being only one race and are non-Hispanic. "In dealing with the police" and "By the criminal justice system" were asked of separate random subsamples of respondents.
Source: Survey of U.S. adults conducted Jan. 22-Feb. 5, 2019.
"Race in America 2019"

PEW RESEARCH CENTER

TRANSFORMATIVE DIALOGUE

When we listen to one another and are open to consider each other's perspectives, transformation can take place. Transformative Dialogue is a reflective learning process in which multiple perspectives are presented, considered, explored and, perhaps, integrated. Participants uncover and examine assumptions and develop shared meaning.

The authors of *A Many Colored Kingdom*[3] cite "Blacks and whites view sources of racial tensions very differently, with whites tending to look at the problems as individualistic and blacks tending to see structural/systemic issues as the primary source." Transformative Dialogue is a disciplined conversation from which meaning evolves collectively through mutual understanding, and non-judgmental acceptance of diverse points of view.

---

[3] Frazier, Elizabeth Conde. *A Many Colored Kingdom*. 2004. Baker Academic

FUNDAMENTAL CONCEPTS

To enable our facilitation of the July 22nd dialogues on race, there are a few fundamental concepts that will enable us to have a shared perspective and deepen our understanding of racism and anti-racism work. It is not expected that you would recite, or even share these concepts with participants. Rather, they are provided to enable us to hear and respond to dialogue participants informatively.

1. **Systemic Racism/Structural Racism/Institutional Racism** are three different ways of referencing the complex interaction of policies, practices and culture that normalize and legitimize protection of unearned privileges for Whites while producing chronic disadvantages for Blacks in every major facet of life; housing, employment, education, health care, criminal justice and more. White privilege is short-hand for systemic racism.

2. The **4 Is of Oppression** is commonly used to delineate how structural racism works. It is an interrelated system based on ideas and stereotypes. Beginning with an *ideology* or belief that Whites are superior to Blacks, *institutions* craft laws, policies, and practices that control others, (police' excessive use of force, hiring policies, sub-prime loans), giving tacit permission for one group to *interpersonally* disrespect another with impunity (Blackface, racist jokes, stereotypes), all of this culminating in *internalization,* by members of the oppressed group, resulting in despair, powerlessness, and even violent aggression. Graphic can be found on page 35.

Systemic racism does not require awareness for it to work for or against you. The unseen belief system, like air, is always present and affects us all. The way the system works is on the belief that racial disparities are the product, not of systems, but of individual behavior. It draws attention to an individual's behavior and primes people to search for the behavior that caused the disparity.

- ○ George Floyd, murdered by police officer, and President Trump retweeted an attack on George Floyd's character by Candace Owens.

- ○ Tamir Rice, killed by police, and police wanted to charge Tamir Rice with inducing panic and aggravated menacing, according to Vox May 21, 2015.

- ○ Ahmaud Arbery killed by a former police officer and son; and there was widespread speculation that Arbery was accused of stealing from a construction site.

- ○ Blacks are jailed at a 6x higher rate for drug charges even though whites use drugs at similar rates.[xxxvi]

- ○ Black male offenders receive 19.1 percent longer sentences for the same crimes that White male offenders commit. [xxxvii]

- ○ Whites overestimate crimes by Black people by 20%-30% based on the belief that Blacks are more criminal than any other identity group.[xxxviii]

3. **Colorblindness** makes the argument that race doesn't matter. It rejects racial categorization and believes that society will make necessary adjustments without intentional, coordinated intervention. "I don't see color," is often heard as a remedy to racism. However, it is antithetical to structural racism, which embeds race and racial discrimination into major facets of life.

Colorblindness supports the myth of meritocracy and guides misguided thinking that anyone, regardless of race or ethnicity, can succeed if they work hard enough. The myth of meritocracy serves as an argument against policies to correct past wrongs with the supposition that if a person of color is not succeeding, it must be due to lack of effort; rather than structural barriers. It is an effective tool for the maintenance of white privilege and a racial hierarchy, because if a Black person is not succeeding, it has to be due to laziness, lack of intelligence, or other negative beliefs (refer back to 4 Is). Robin DiAngelo states it is pointless to ask the binary question; is this or isn't this racist? It is more appropriate to acknowledge that race plays a role in our interactions. The better question is: *how* does race play a role in this?

4. **Implicit Bias** refers to automatically activated attitudes and stereotypes outside conscious awareness that affect people's perceptions, actions and decisions. © 2021

Hold on to these four fundamental schools of thought, as we consider building anti-racist structures to achieve desired outcomes of equity and the beloved community.

Want to learn more about structural racism

1. Watch video: <u>**The Disturbing History of the Suburbs**</u> | **Adam Ruins Everything** (6:19 minutes)
2. Listen to Dr. Tricia Rose, Brown University, July 2017 "How structural racism works." https://youtu.be/KT1vsOJctMk
3. Read article in USA Today by N'dea Yancey-Bragg – "What is Systemic Racism? Here's what it means and How You Can Help Dismantle it." https://www.usatoday.com/story/news/nation/2020/06/15/systemic-racism-what-does-mean/5343549002/

ESTABLISHING A POSTIVE ATMOSPHERE FOR PARTICIPANTS

"Seek first to understand before seeking to be understood."
Stephen Covey

An effective dialogue offers participants the opportunity to:

- Listen and be listened to so that all speakers can be heard.
- Speak and be spoken to in a respectful manner.
- Develop or deepen mutual understanding.
- Learn about the perspectives of others and reflect on one's own views.

FACILITATOR'S ROLE

The dialogue facilitator has a responsibility to the group as a whole, while also considering each person's individuality and level of comfort. You don't need to be an "expert" or even the most knowledgeable person in the group on the topic discussed, however, you should be the best prepared for the discussion. Know your material and know yourself. You may choose to have a script or an outline or you may choose to memorize what you want to say. I am a fan of jazz, so no matter what you decide, once the dialogue begins, allow improvisation. In other words, go with the flow.

The dialogue facilitator's role is vital to the success of the dialogue. It requires a high level of alertness and awareness, as well as keen listening skills and humility, knowing when not to talk. Less is more; speak when you need to but err on the side of encouraging participants to speak. There is no right way to facilitate; you must find the style that makes you both comfortable and confident. If you're at ease, the participants will be influenced by that.

Co-Facilitators

"Our goal is to draw on participants' experiences, not opinions. Opinions tend to elicit defensiveness, while shared experiences elicit curiosity."

Peggy McIntosh

73

- Communicate often to one another before, during and after session.
- Share responsibility and take turns acting as the lead facilitator.
- Support one another

Facilitator Responsibilities

Establish an open and welcoming environment.

Practice active listening; paraphrase content and feeling expressed by participants.

Build on what participants offer, but avoid lecturing.

Respond to questions in a manner that fosters dialogue.

Know your material.

Stay on track with agenda and time frame

What Happens In Breakout Rooms?

A Breakout Room welcomes participants to a small group and sets a relaxed tone. Remind them that the purpose is to listen to and learn from each other. Your role is to foster brave spaces for conversations about racism and anti-racism that are grounded in mutual respect. Make sure everyone can hear you. If you're not sure, ask.

"Welcome, thank you for coming today. My name is xxx and I am delighted to be here and look forward to our time together." Second Facilitator greets the group. "Our goal today is to maintain a stance of neutrality and to keep the dialogue flowing. Facilitate listening to and learning from each other. Your active engagement is essential to our achieving that goal. We encourage you to be open minded, take risks and engage."

Set expectations

"There is a direct correlation between what you put into a session like this and what you get out of it. Contribute a little, get a little. Contribute a lot, you get more. For some of you, this may be the first time you've engaged in a group conversation on this topic; let's approach it as if we are in a laboratory: try some things out, allow and forgive mistakes, assume good intent. Try again. We hope this initial conversation will whet your appetite for more. Anti-racism is a vast topic and we look forward to hearing from each of you, yet we know, given the time we have, much will be left unsaid. During the time we have together in our breakout rooms, we will cover four items, introduction, agreements, to make sure we get the most out of the dialogue, and two questions about race and anti-racism. Then we will return to the large group to share ..."

Establish agreements

"To help us authentically engage in the conversation, we'd like to offer some agreements. Your commitment to these agreements will help us have a R.E.A.L. conversation."

Responsibility   Take responsibility for maintaining a learning stance.
Use "I" messages – speak from your perspective, share your own experiences.
No blaming/shaming – Don't assume, assign intentions, beliefs or opinions to what others say – if unclear, ask.

Engage   Participate in a way that encourages dialogue.
                Resist binary thinking ('that's right/wrong).
                Think in questions (what about; under what
                conditions could that be true? where might
                that occur?)
                Don't talk too much/too little.

Agree to Disagree agreeably
                Be willing to remain in the conversation, even
                if you don't agree with all the participants/
                perspectives
                Release your certainty – be willing to
                challenge your own perspective/position
                Address controversy with civility

Lean & Listen   Pay attention to your feelings. Rather than
                withdraw, lean into the discomfort and ask
                yourself: "what am I feeling?" "Why am I
                feeling this way?"
                Listen with curiosity, for surprises
                Help each other become better listeners
                (paraphrase, inquire)

Finally, maintain confidentiality –

Stories shared here, stay here. Peoples' stories are for them to tell. Certainly, share your own story, but not anyone else's without permission.

What you learn here leaves here. Please share widely, your insights about racism and anti-racism as a result of your experience.

Ask participants if they agree with maintaining confidentiality. What else do you need to feel comfortable sharing your ideas and experiences today? Then let's get going.

Participant introductions

"Please share two things; your name & how long you've lived in the Attleboro community."

Dialogue Questions

Frame the questions to help participants delve into them. Begin with "Kendi says: 'The heartbeat of racism is denial. The heartbeat of anti-racism is confession."

Question One*: "When was the first time you became aware of your race? Please share your story or experience."*

Question Two: "In what ways have you noticed that race matters in society?" What is the distinction between non-racist and anti-racist?"

a. Move the group through the dialogue format, keeping an eye on time.

b. Help group members identify areas of agreement and disagreement.

c. It's helpful to occasionally restate the key question or insight under discussion.

d. Draw out points of view that haven't surfaced.

e. Follow and focus the conversation, and help to clarify the discussion.

f. Summarize themes in the discussion or ask others to do so.

Close the dialogue: Give participants a chance to talk about the most important thing they gained from the discussion. You may ask them to share any new ideas or thoughts they've had as a result of the discussion. Encourage them to think about what worked and what didn't, and to share their insights on their evaluation forms.

Key Facilitation Skills

"Accepting" shows respect for each participant in the group. Make it clear that dialogue involves no "right" or "wrong" responses. One way to show acceptance and respect is to briefly summarize what is heard, and to convey the feeling with which it was shared. Reflecting both the content and the feeling lets the person know that she or he has been heard. For example, you might say "It sounds like you felt hurt when you were slighted by someone of a different race." Once in a while ask participants to sum up the most important points that have come out in the discussion. This gives the group a sense of accomplishment and a point of reference for more sharing.

- **Notice** who is not speaking and give everyone a chance to contribute; "Let's hear from someone who hasn't spoken yet."
- **Reflecting** – Feeding back the content and feeling of participants' comments. "Let me see if I'm hearing you correctly..."
- **Clarifying** – Rephrasing an idea or thought to make it clearer. "What I believe I hear you saying is..."
- **Summarizing** – Stating the main themes concisely.
- **Remaining neutral** while encouraging participants to explore all facets of their own and others' opinions
- **Shifting Focus** – Transitioning from one speaker or topic to another. "Thank you, James. Do you have anything to add, Sherry?" "We've been focusing on views 1 and 2 does anyone have strong feelings about view 3?"
- **Using Silence** – Allowing time and space for reflection by pausing between comments. Respect the silence – don't panic when people are quiet, often they are thinking, not resisting.

MANAGING PARTICIPANTS AND QUESTIONS

Problem	Ineffective Response	Facilitative Response
Various perspectives	Try to gain consensus	With care and humility, try to draw out multiple perspectives. Ask, "Can you say more about that?" "When you say XX, what do you mean?"
Contradictions from same participant	Call them out	Contradictions can be an indication of new learning. Affirm the value of open-mindedness resulting in new understanding and a changed view.
Silence	Fill it in	Rest in the silence. Don't interrupt it – simply wait
Conflict between two participants	Take sides	Focus on issues and not persons, "what is it about the idea that's causing such a strong reaction?"
Participant becomes emotional	Redirect all attention to the participant	Often, a participant's emotions help to move the group to a deeper level of discussion. Take your lead from the participant, perhaps ask, "Do you need anything right now, or is it ok for us to continue?"

Answering Questions

Responding to Questions that Aim to Gather Information

Most questions represent legitimate requests for information or clarification as people attempt to grasp an issue. In these cases, use the following as a guide:

- Determine if the *timing* is right for an immediate response.
    - If the question fits in where you are in the agenda, answer it at that time.
    - If it anticipates something coming up later, tell the questioner you will be getting to that and ask if they would mind holding onto the question temporarily. (If the response can be quick, go ahead and respond – questioners *can* get annoyed if asked to wait.)
    - If it seems unrelated to the current topic, suggest that they speak to you "offline" later.

Responding to Questions that Aim to Express Feelings

Questions may indicate resistance from your audience, either to the material, the way it is being presented, or the underlying issues. Sometimes people ask questions that are really challenges in disguise. While these expressions *may* be an indication of how the questioner is reacting to either the facilitator or the material, generally the questions are indications of issues that have surfaced for the questioner. As a facilitator, your task is then to keep the discussion on track, maintain participants' interest and energy and keep your cool. The following suggestions can help you do that:

- **Listen for the underlying feelings** behind what the person is saying as well as the content.

80

- **Decide whether to discuss or deflect.** Decide whether further exploration of the question will enhance the discussion. If you think it would be risky or inappropriate to focus on it, politely steer the conversation back to where you want it to be. For example, you might say "I hear your frustration with the whole issue of [white privilege], and it is an important issue. Unfortunately, we can't give that discussion the time and attention it needs during this brief session, but I encourage you to create other opportunities to have those conversations. I'd love to talk with you more about that when we finish tonight."

- **Respond, but don't react.** Avoid fueling the questioner's feelings by denying, ignoring or downplaying them (which can also alienate other participants). Let the speaker know they have been heard. Above all, keep your tone and attitude positive and supportive.

===

[i] DuBois, W.E.B. "Prayer for Dark People," as cited in *Standing in the Need of Prayer: A Celebration of Black Prayer, ed. Schomburg Center for Research in Black Culture and Coretta Scott King*. New York, Free Press-Simon & Schuster. 2003 p. 45

[ii] Emerson, M. *People of The Dream*. New Jersey, Princeton University Press. New Jersey. 2006. "The word 'indigenous' in America is usually associated with Native Americans. They are indigenous people, and their culture is indigenous to the land. I speak here not of land but of the political entity called the United States. There are two "home-grown" cultures raised up within the political entity called the United States. It is in this respect that I use the term indigenous to refer to black and white culture."

[iii] Buber, M. used the term dialogue in 1914 to describe a mode of exchange among human beings in which there is a true turning to one another and a full appreciation of another, not as an object in a social function, but as a genuine being.

[iv] Senge, P., Ross, R., Smith, B., Roberts, C., Kleiner, A. *The Fifth Discipline Fieldbook: Strategies and Tools for Building a Learning* Organization. New York, Doubleday. 1994. p. 359

[v] Agree to disagree agreeably by trying on new perspectives and avoiding debate.

[vi] Freire, P. *Education for Critical Consciousness*. New York, Bloomsbury Publishing. 1974.

[vii] "Diversity Training Curriculum Center for Youth and Communities." Waltham, Heller School, Brandeis University and Commonwealth of Massachusetts Office of Work/Life Diversity. June, 2018. p.9

viii Freire, P. Pedagogy of the Oppressed. New York, Continuum International. 1970.

ix Boyes-Watson, C., Pranis, K. (Adapted from) Circle Forward Resource Guide. Boston, The Center for Restorative Justice. Suffolk University. 2010.

x Nellis, A. (2016) "The Color of Justice: Racial and Ethnic Disparity in State Prisons." The Sentencing Project. 2016. Sentencingproject.org.

xi King, M. L. "I Have a Dream." March on Washington. The Washington Mall. Washington, DC. 8/28/1963.

xii www.povertyusa.org/facts

xiii https://wholads.us/electedofficials

xiv Diangelo, R. White Fragility: Why it's So Hard for White People to Talk About Racism. Boston, Beacon Press. 2018. p. 143

xv Powell, J. leads the UC Berkeley Othering & Belonging Institute and holds the Robert D. Haas Chancellor's Chair in Equity and Inclusion, Professor of Law and Professor of African American Studies and Ethnic Studies at the University of California, Berkeley School of Law.

xvi Conde-Frazier, E., Kang, S., Parrett, G. Many Colored Kingdom: Multiracial Dynamics for Spiritual Formation. Grand Rapids, Baker Publishing Group. 2004

xvii Ibid. p. 10

xviii Emerson, M. People of the Dream. Princeton, Princeton University Press. 2006.

xix Ibid. p 619

xx Ibid. p 619

xxi https://www.nytimes.com/2021/10/11/sports/football/what-did-jon-gruden-say.html

xxii Pace, C. *Freedom Faith: The Womanist Vision of Prathia Hall*. Athens, The University of Georgia Press. 2019.

xxiii Emerson, M. *People of The Dream*. Princeton, Princeton University Press. 2006.

xxiv Edwards, K. *The Elusive Dream*: The Power of Race in Interracial Churches. New York, Oxford University Press. 2008.

xxv Emerson, M. *People of the Dream*. Princeton, Princeton University Press. 2006. p. 139

xxvi Du Bois, W.E.B. *The Souls of Black Folk*. Chicago, A. C. McClurg & Company. 1903.

xxvii Ibid, p. 3

xxviii Bonilla-Silva, E. (2003, as cited in Mazzocca, P. 2006). "The Dangers of Not Speaking About Race. A Summary of Research Affirming the Merits of a Color Conscious Approach to Racial Communication and Equity." Columbus, Kirwan Institute for the Study of Race and Ethnicity | The Ohio State University. p. 4

xxix Lingenfelter, S., & Mayers, M. *Ministering Cross-Culturally An Incarnational Model for Personal Relationships*. Grand Rapids, Baker Book House. 1992.

xxx Pui-Lan, K. *Postcolonial Imagination and Feminist Theology*. Louisville, Westminster-John Knox Press. 2005. P. 17

[xxxi] Frost, R. "Mending Wall" www.poetryfoundation.org

[xxxii] New Revised Standard Version. Matthew 22:37-29. Luke 10:27. Leviticus 19:18. Deut. 6:5. Oxford, Oxford University Press. 2001.

[xxxiii] https://onha.yale.edu/

[xxxiv] Ibid

[xxxv] Isaacs, W. *Dialogue And The Art of Thinking Together*. New York, Doubleday. 1999.

[xxxvi] https://naacp.org/resources/criminal-justice-fact-sheet

[xxxvii] 2017 Demographic Differences in Sentencing: An Update to the 2012 Booker Report. U. S. Sentencing Commission https://www.ussc.gov/sites/default/files/pdf/research-and-publications/research-publications/2017/20171114_Demographics.pdf

[xxxviii] https://www.sentencingproject.org/wp-content/uploads/2015/11/Race-and-Punishment.pdf

BIBLIOGRAPHY

1. Alinksy, S. D. Reveille for Radicals. New York, Vintage Books. 1989.

2. Bache, E. Culture Clash. Wilmington, Banks Channel Books. 1989

3. Banaji, M., & Greenwald, A. Blindspot: Hidden Biases of Good People. New York, Delacorte Press. 2013.

4. Bennett, L. Before the Mayflower: A History of the Negro in America 1619-1964. (Revised edition). Middlesex, Penguin Books. 1962.

5. Blank, R. & Slipp, S. voices of diversity: Real People Talk about Problems and Solutions in a Workplace Where Everyone is Not Alike. New York, American Management Association. 1994.

6. Bonilla-Silva, E. racism without racists: color-blind racism and the persistence of racial inequality in America. Lanham, Rowman & Littlefield Publishing Group. 2006

7. Brown, M., Carnoy, M. Currie, E., Duster, T., Oppenheimer, D., Shultz, M., Wellman, D. White-Washing Race: The Myth of a Color-Blind Society. Berkeley, University of California Press. 2005.

8. Cekic, O. Overcoming Hate Through Dialogue: Confronting Prejudice, Racism, and Bigotry with Conversation ---and Coffee. Coral Gables, Mango Publishing. 2020.

9. Chugh, D. The Person You Mean to Be: How Good People Fight Bias. New York, Harper Collins. 2018.

10. Coates, T-N. Between The World And Me. Melbourne, The Text Publishing Company. 2015.

11. Diangelo, R. White Fragility: Why it's So Hard for White People to Talk About Racism. Boston, Beacon Press. 2018.

12. Dyson, M. E. The Tears We Cannot Stop. New York, St. Martin's Press. 2017.

13. Eberhardt, J. L. Biased: Uncovering the Hidden Prejudice That Shapes What We See Think, and Do. New York. Viking. 2019.

14. Edwards, K. The Elusive Dream: The Power of Race in Interracial Churches. Oxford, Oxford University Press. 2008.

15. Emerson, M. O., & Woo, R. M. People of the Dream: Multiracial Congregations in the United States. Woodstock, Princeton University Press. 2006.

16. Emerson, M., Yancey, G. Transcending Racial Barriers Toward a Mutual Obligations Approach. Oxford, Oxford University Press. 2011.

17. Esty, K., Griffin, R., & Hirsch, M. S. A Manager's Guide to Solving Problems and Turning Diversity into a Competitive Advantage: Workplace Diversity. Holbrook, Adams Media Corporation. 1995.

18. Fletcher, J. K. Disappearing Acts: Gender, Power, and Relational Practice at Work. Cambridge, The MIT Press. 2001.

19. Freire, P. Pedagogy of the oppressed. New York, Continuum. 2003.

20. Gilligan, C. In A Different Voice: Psychological Theory and Women's Development. Cambridge, Harvard University Press. 1993.

21. Gladwell, M. Blink: The Power of Thinking Without Thinking. New York, Little, Brown and Company. 2005.

22. Gladwell, M. Outliers: The Story of Success. New York. Little, Brown and Company. 2008.

23. Greenberg, E., & Weber, K. Generation WE: How Millennial Youth Are Taking Over America and Changing Our World Forever. Emeryville, Pachatusan. 2008.

24. Gumbs, A. Undrowned: Black Feminist Lessons from Marine Mammals. Chico, A. K. Press. 2020.

25. Hamlin, W. T. The Chains of Psychological Slavery: The Mental Illness of Racism. Silver Springs, The Institute for Child and Family Psychiatry, Inc. 1979

26. Hammond, Z. Culturally Responsive Teaching & The Brain: Promoting Authentic Engagement and Rigor Among Culturally and Linguistically Diverse Students. Thousand Oaks, Corwin. 2015.

27. Hendricks, O. The Politics of Jesus: Rediscovering the True Revolutionary Nature of Jesus' Teachings and How they Have Been Corrupted. New York, Doubleday. 2006.

28. Henze, R., Katz, A., Norte, E., Sather, S., & Walker, E. Leading for Diversity: How School Leaders Promote Positive Interethnic Relations. Thousand Oaks, Corwin. 2002.

29. Hicks, D. Leading with Dignity: How to Create a Culture that Brings out the Best in People. New Haven, Yale University Press. 2018.

30. Hofstede, G. "Geert Hofstede on Culture." YouTube https:// youtu.be/wdh40kgyYOY October 22, 2011.

31. Ignatiev, N. How the Irish Became White. New York, Routledge. 1995.

32. Irving, D. Waking Up White: And Finding Myself in the Story of Race. Cambridge, Elephant Room Press. 2014.

33. Jones, Robert P. White Too Long: The Legacy of White Supremacy in American Christianity. New York, Simon & Schuster. 2020

34. Kendi, I. How to Be an Anti-Racist. New York, Random House. 2019.

35. King, R. Mindful of Race: Transforming Racism from the Inside Out. Boulder, Sounds True. 2018.

36. Law, E. Inclusion: Making Room for Grace. St. Louis, Chalice Press. 2000.

37. Law, E. The Wolf Shall Dwell with the Lamb: A Spirituality for Leadership in a Multicultural Community. St. Louis, Chalice Press. 1993.

38. Lindsey, R., Robins, K., & Terrell, R. Cultural Proficiency: A Manual for School Leaders. Thousand Oaks, Corwin. 2009.

39. Livingston, R. The Conversation: How Seeking and Speaking the Truth About Racism Can Radically Transform Individuals and Organizations. New York, Random House. 2021

40. Loden, M., & Rosener, J. Workforce America!: Managing Employee Diversity as a Vital Resource. Homewood, Business One Irwin. 1991.

41. Lorde, A. Sister Outsider. Berkeley, Crossing Press. 2007.

42. Mazel, E. "And don't call me a racist!": A treasury of quotes on the past, present and future of the color line in America. Lexington, Argonaut Press.1998.

43. McClure, D. Freckles Presents We Love You Mama. Malden, Colonial Printing Company. 1979.

44. McClure, D. Freckles. Falmouth, Kendall Printing Company. 1976.

45. McMickle, M. Let the Oppressed Go Free: Exploring Theologies of Liberation. Valley Forge, Judson Press. 2020

46. Patterson, K., Grenny, J., Maxfield, D., McMillan, R., Switzler, A. Crucial Accountability: Tools for Resolving Violated Expectations, Broken Commitments, and Bad Behavior. New York, McGraw Hill. 2013.

47. Patterson. K., Grenny, J., McMillan, R., Switzler, A. Crucial Conversations: Tools for Talking When Stakes Are High. New York, McGraw Hill. 2012.

48. Patterson. K., Grenny, J., McMillan, R., Switzler, A. Crucial Confrontations: Tools for Resolving Broken Promises, Violated Expectations, and Bad Behavior. New York, McGraw Hill. 2005.

49. Pegues, J. Black and Blue: Inside the Divide Between the Police and Black America. Amherst, Prometheus Books. 2017.

50. Petersen W., Novak M., & Gleason, P. Concepts of Ethnicity: dimensions of ethnicity. Cambridge, The Belknap Press.1980.

51. Pollock, M. Every Day Anti-Racism: Getting Real About Race in School. New York, The New Press. 2008.

52. Pranis, K. The Little Book of Circle Processes. Intercourse, Good Books. 2005.

53. Reynolds, J., & Kendi, I. Stamped Racism, Antiracism, and You. New York, Little, Brown and Company. 2020.

54. Roberts, L., & Mayo, A. "Advancing Black Leaders: African Americans are Still Vastly Underrepresented in Many US Organizations. Here's A Roadmap for Change." Harvard Business Review. BG 1906. November 2019. pp. 1-10

55. Rodriguez, R. Brown: The Last Discovery of America. New York, Viking. 2002.

56. Schirch, L., Campt, D. The Little Book of Dialogue for Difficult Subjects: A Practical, Hands-On Guide. New York, Good Books. 2007

57. Senge, P., Keliner, A., Roberts, C., Ross, R., & Smith, B. The Fifth Discipline Fieldbook: Strategies and Tools for Building A Learning Organization. New York, Doubleday Dell Publishing Group. 1994.

58. Singleton, G. Courageous Conversations About Race: A Field Guide for Achieving Equity in Schools. Thousand Oaks, Corwin. 2015.

59. Smith, D., Frey, N., Pumpian, I., & Fisher, D. Building Equity: Policies and Practices to Empower All Learners. Alexandria, ASCD. 2017.

60. Steinhorn, L., & Diggs-Brown, B. By the Color of our Skin: The Illusion of Integration and the Reality of Race. New York, Plume. 1999.

61. Suarez, R. The Old Neighborhood: What We Lose in the Great Suburban Migration: 1966-1999. New York. The Free Press. 1999.

62. Takaki, R. A Different Mirror: A History of Multicultural America. Boston, Little, Brown and Company. 1993.

63. Tannen, D. Talking From 9 to 5 Women and Men in the Workplace: Language, Sex and Power. New York, Avon Books. 1994.

64. Thandeka. Learning to be White: Money, Race and God in America. New York, Continuum. 2006.

65. Vitale, A. The End of Policing. New York, Verso. 2017.

66. Volf, M. Exclusion & Embrace: A Theological Exploration of Identity, Otherness, and Reconciliation. Nashville, Abingdon Press. 1996.

67. Wah, Mun, L. The Art of Mindful Facilitation. Berkeley, Stir Fry Seminars and Consulting. 2004.

68. Wilson, D. "Yale and New Haven Find Common Ground." New York Times. December 16, 2007.

69. Wilson, M., Hoppe, M., & Sayles, L. Managing Across Cultures: A Learning Framework. Greensboro, Center for Creative Leadership.1996.

70. Zinn, H. A People's History of the United States. New York, Harper Perennial Modern Classics. 2005.